Table of Co

The Jean Paré Story

Jean Paré (pronounced "jeen PAIR-ee") grew up understanding that the combination of family, friends and home cooking is the best recipe for a good life. When Jean left home, she took with her a love of cooking, many family recipes and an intriguing desire to read cookbooks as if they were novels!

"Never share a recipe you wouldn't use yourself."

When her four children had all reached school age, Jean volunteered to cater the 50th anniversary celebration of the Vermilion School of Agriculture, now Lakeland College, in Alberta, Canada. Working from her home, Jean prepared a dinner for more than 1,000 people and from there launched a flourishing catering operation that continued for more than 18 years.

As requests for her recipes increased, Jean was often asked, "Why don't you write a cookbook?" The release of *150 Delicious Squares* on April 14, 1981, marked the debut of what would soon turn into one of the world's most popular cookbook series.

Company's Coming cookbooks are distributed in Canada, the United States, Australia and other world markets. Bestsellers many times over in English, Company's Coming cookbooks have also been published in French and Spanish.

Familiar and trusted in home kitchens around the world, Company's Coming cookbooks are offered in a variety of formats. Highly regarded as kitchen workbooks, the softcover Original Series, with its lay-flat plastic comb binding, is still a favourite among home cooks.

Jean Paré's approach to cooking has always called for quick and easy recipes using everyday ingredients. That view served her well, and the tradition continues in the Practical Gourmet series.

Jean's Golden Rule of Cooking is: Never share a recipe you wouldn't use yourself. It's an approach that has worked—millions of times over!

The Slow Cooker

The slow cooker can be your best friend in the kitchen. With a little advance planning, you can set everything up before you leave the house in the morning and come home to a meal that is ready to eat as soon as you walk through the door. Sounds great, right? Not so fast…

The general misconception about slow cookers is that if you toss everything into the pot and walk away, you'll come back to a sumptuous, perfectly prepared meal. Not true! As with any type of cooking, slow cookers have rules for getting the best results. If you don't follow the rules or skip some steps and simply toss your ingredients into the pot willy-nilly, you are likely to come home to an unappetizing bowl of slop.

So here's a list of slow cooker dos and don'ts to ensure your adventures in slow cooking are efficient, successful and delicious.

• Start with the right type of recipe. Not all foods are meant to be cooked in a slow cooker. Choose dishes that benefit from a long, slow cooking times, such as tougher cuts of meat, stews, chili and curries. Save the more delicate foods, such as most types of fish and seafood as well as many soft vegetables, or foods you want to be crispy, such as a chicken with the skin on, for the oven or frying pan.

- Do not overcook your dish! Just because you *can* cook a recipe for 8 or more hours in a slow cooker doesn't mean you should. Follow recipe directions carefully and use your machine's timer if you plan to be away from your slow cooker longer than the recipe's recommended cooking time.

- In a slow cooker, the heat is most intense at the bottom of the pot, so layer your ingredients accordingly. Items that take the longest to cook should be at the bottom, closest to the heat source, and more delicate foods that require less cooking time should be near the top of the pot so they do not overcook and become mushy.

- Fill your slow cooker no more than two-thirds full; otherwise, your meal will take longer to cook, and it could boil over the sides of the machine as it cooks, taking away from the overall quality of the dish and leaving you with a mess to clean up.

- Do not cook frozen meat in your slow cooker. Because slow cooker temperatures are so low, the meat may stay at the temperature "danger zone" for too long, allowing bacteria to multiply and ultimately leading to food poisoning.

- In most cases, it is a good idea to brown your meat before starting the slow cooking process. Not only does the browning step improve the overall flavour of the dish, it also allows some of the fat to be rendered and drained so your finished product is not as greasy.

- Milk products tend not to fare well in the slow cooker and should be added near the end of the cooking time.

- Pasta and rice should either be added near the end of the cooking time or cooked in a separate pot and added to the dish just before serving to prevent them from becoming mushy or gummy.

- Hardy vegetables, such as sweet potatoes or other root vegetables, can be added early on, but delicate vegetables such as summer squash and peppers should be added in the last 30 or so minutes of cooking time so they maintain some textural integrity. This is the best time to add fresh herbs, too.

- Go easy on the wine (or other spirits). Alcohol does not burn off in the slow cooker and can overpower your dish if you add too much. Also, it's best to use a good quality wine. The slow cooker is not the place to use up the open bottle that has been languishing in your fridge. If you don't like the flavor of the wine that goes into the slow cooker, you won't like the flavour of the dish that comes out.

- No peeking! As your meal cooks and begins to fill your home with tantalizing aromas, you may be tempted to lift the slow cooker's lid and check on its progress. Resist the urge. Every time you lift the lid, you release some of the built-up heat and moisture, which can add as much as 30 minutes to the cooking time. Only lift the lid early if you are adding ingredients that require a shorter cooking time, such as milk products, softer vegetables or fresh herbs, and then add all the new ingredients at one time so the lid only has to come off once.

Mexi Dip

Serve this layered dip with tortilla or pita chips. If you like a little more spice, use hot salsa and increase the amount of chili powder.

Light cream cheese, softened	16 oz.	500 g
Finely chopped cooked ham	1/2 cup	125 mL
Grated medium Cheddar cheese	3 cups	750 mL
Medium or hot salsa	1/2 cup	125 mL
Can of chopped green chillies (4 oz., 114 mL), drained	1	1
Chili powder	1/2 tsp.	2 mL

Mash cream cheese with a fork in a medium bowl. Spread in bottom of a 3 quart (3L) slow cooker. Sprinkle ham evenly over top. Sprinkle with Cheddar cheese.

Stir salsa and green chilies together in a small bowl. Spoon over cheese. Sprinkle with chili powder. Cook, covered, on Low for 2 to 2 1/2 hours until warmed through. Do not stir. Makes 4 cups (1 L).

1 tbsp (15 mL): 40 Calories; 3 g Total Fat (1 g Mono, 0 g Poly, 2 g Sat); 10 mg Cholesterol; 0 g Carbohydrate (0 g Fibre, 0 g Sugar); 2 g Protein; 80 mg Sodium

Did you add a few too many chili peppers (or chili powder) to your recipe than your mouth can handle? Try dousing that fire with a glass of milk. Dairy products contain a protein called casein that helps neutralize the fiery burn caused by the capsaicin in all forms of chili peppers.

Beefy Chip Dip

Thick, meaty and cheesy, this dip is perfect with pita or tortilla chips. It would also make a great topping for nachos!

Lean ground beef	1 lb.	454 g
Grated Monterey Jack cheese	3 cups	750 mL
Worcestershire sauce	2 tsp.	10 mL
Can of chopped green chilies	1	1
(4 oz., 114 mL)		
Medium or hot salsa	1 cup	250 mL
Chili powder	1/2 tsp.	2 mL
Onion powder	1/2 tsp.	2 mL

Scramble-fry ground beef in a non-stick frying pan until no longer pink. Drain. Use fork to break up any lumps and transfer to your slow cooker.

Stir in next 6 ingredients. Cook, covered, on Low for 1 3/4 to 2 hours, stirring occasionally, until warmed through. Makes 4 cups (1 L).

1 tbsp (15 mL): 40 Calories; 3 g Total Fat (1 g Mono, 0 g Poly, 1.5 g Sat); 9 mg Cholesterol; 0 g Carbohydrate (0 g Fibre, 0 g Sugar); 3 g Protein; 65 mg Sodium

ᑫᐱ Despite its British-sounding name, Worcestershire sauce is Indian in origin. The recipe was brought to Worcester from Bengal by the English Lord Sandys in 1835. He asked the now-famous chemists John Lea and William Perrins to make up a batch of the sauce he had so enjoyed on his travels. Lea and Perrins found the end result to be completely inedible but, wasting naught, they stashed a barrel of it in the basement. A year or two later they rediscovered the barrel, sampled the contents and found that it had mellowed into a very tasty sauce. In 1838, the partners began to sell the sauce commercially. It was an instant success. The original recipe remains a secret but probably contains vinegar, sugar, soy sauce, tamarind, lime, cloves and anchovies among other ingredients. Even today, Worcestershire sauce is aged in barrels for several years before it is deemed fit for human consumption.

Cranberry Chili Meatballs

This recipe makes about 4 dozen meatballs, making it a perfect choice for a potluck or other get together; or you can divide the meatballs into portions and freeze them for an easy weekday supper. The bite from the chili sauce complements the sweet cranberry flavour and savoury meatballs. Serve over rice or with a baguette.

Large eggs, fork-beaten	4	4
Milk	1 cup	250 mL
Finely chopped onion	1/2 cup	125 mL
Dry bread crumbs	2 cups	500 mL
Worcestershire sauce	4 tsp.	20 mL
Salt	4 tsp.	20 mL
Pepper	1 tsp.	5 mL
Lean ground beef	4 lbs.	1.8 kg
Ketchup	1/2 cup	125 mL
Chili sauce	1/2 cup	125 mL
Cranberry jelly	1 cup	250 mL
White vinegar	1 tsp.	5 mL

Combine eggs, milk, onion, bread crumbs, Worcestershire sauce, salt and pepper in a large bowl. Stir until well blended. Mix in ground beef. Shape into 1 1/2 inch (3.8 cm) balls (see Tip, below). Arrange on a greased baking sheet. Bake in 425°F (220°C) oven for 15 to 16 minutes until no pink remains.

Combine remaining 4 ingredients in your slow cooker. Add meatballs and stir gently. Cook, covered, on Low for 8 to 10 hours or on High for 4 to 5 hours. Makes about 96 meatballs. Makes 16 servings.

1 serving: 430 Calories; 18 g Total Fat (8 g Mono, 1 g Poly, 7 g Sat); 115 mg Cholesterol; 32 g Carbohydrate (2 g Fibre, 14 g Sugar); 27 g Protein; 1190 mg Sodium

Tip: For uniform meatballs either use a scoop or press the beef mixture into a square or rectangle shape that is the same thickness all over. Cut into smaller squares and roll each square into a ball.

Asian Chicken Wings

These wings marinate in the sauce as they cook, making every bite loaded with flavour.

Whole chicken wings (or drumettes)	**3 lbs.**	**1.4 kg**
Soy sauce	**1 cup**	**250 mL**
Brown sugar, packed	**3/4 cup**	**175 mL**
Water	**1/2 cup**	**125 mL**
Lemon juice	**1 tsp.**	**5 mL**
Dry mustard	**1/4 tsp.**	**1 mL**
Garlic powder	**1/4 tsp.**	**1 mL**
Salt	**1/2 tsp.**	**2 mL**
Ground ginger	**1/4 tsp.**	**1 mL**

Discard tips and cut wings apart at joint. Place pieces in your slow cooker.

Combine remaining 8 ingredients in a bowl. Pour over chicken pieces. Cook, covered, on Low for 8 to 9 hours or on High for 4 to 4 1/2 hours until tender. Serve from slow cooker or remove to a platter. Makes about 28 wing pieces or about 18 drumettes.

1 wing piece (with sauce): 150 Calories; 8 g Total Fat (3.5 g Mono, 2 g Poly, 2.5 g Sat); 35 mg Cholesterol; 7 g Carbohydrate (0 g Fibre, 6 g Sugar); 12 g Protein; 690 mg Sodium

Beef Minestrone

When your day away from home is long, this comforting dish will be ready and waiting for your return.

Beef stew meat, diced	1/2 lb.	225 g
Can of tomatoes (14 oz., 398 mL), with juice, broken up	1	1
Beef broth	1 cup	250 mL
Chopped onion	1 cup	250 mL
Grated cabbage	1 cup	250 mL
Medium carrot, diced or thinly sliced	1	1
Celery stalk, diced or thinly sliced	1	1
Medium potato, diced	1	1
Cut green beans	1/2 cup	125 mL
Parsley flakes	1 tsp.	5 mL
Garlic powder	1/4 tsp.	1 mL
Dried sweet basil	1/4 tsp.	1 mL
Dried whole oregano	1/4 tsp.	1 mL
Salt	1 1/2 tsp.	7 mL
Pepper	1/4 tsp.	1 mL
Water	4 cups	1 L
Can of white kidney beans (14 oz., 398 mL), drained	1	1
Uncooked elbow macaroni	1/2 cup	125 mL

Grated Parmesan cheese, as a garnish

Combine first 16 ingredients in your slow cooker. Stir well. Cook, covered, on Low for 10 to 12 hours or on High for 5 to 6 hours.

Turn heat to High. Add kidney beans and macaroni. Cook, covered, for 15 to 20 minutes until macaroni is tender.

Garnish with cheese to serve. Makes 10 1/2 cups (2.6 L).

1 cup (250 mL): 130 Calories; 2.5 g Total Fat (1 g Mono, 0 g Poly, 1 g Sat); 10 mg Cholesterol; 17 g Carbohydrate (5 g Fibre, 3 g Sugar); 9 g Protein; 850 mg Sodium

Chinese Mushroom Soup

A mingling of light ingredients, reminiscent of hot and sour soup. As a variation replace the pork with the same amount of diced cooked beef, chicken or shrimp. For a meatless soup, use the same amount of diced tofu.

Chinese dried mushrooms, stems removed	15	15
Prepared chicken broth	6 cups	1.5 L
Chopped cabbage	1 cup	250 mL
Can of sliced water chestnuts (8 oz., 227 mL), drained	1	1
Can of bamboo shoots (8 oz., 227 mL), drained	1	1
Rice vinegar	1/3 cup	75 mL
Soy sauce	1/4 cup	60 mL
Dried crushed chilies	1 tsp.	5 mL
Diced cooked pork	1 cup	250 mL
Sliced green onion	2 tbsp.	30 mL

Place mushrooms in a small bowl. Add boiling water until it is 2 inches (5 cm) above mushrooms and let stand for about 20 minutes until softened. Drain. Thinly slice mushrooms and transfer to your slow cooker.

Stir in next 6 ingredients. Cook, covered, on Low for 8 to 10 hours or on High for 4 to 5 hours.

Stir in pork and onion. Cook, covered, on High for 10 to 15 minutes until pork is heated through. Makes about 8 cups (2 L).

1 cup (250 mL): 117 Calories; 4 g Total Fat (2 g Mono, .5 g Poly, 1.5 g Sat); 10 mg Cholesterol; 12 g Carbohydrate (2 g Fibre, 4 g Sugar); 14 g Protein; 1720 mg Sodium

Sausage White Bean Soup

A kaleidoscope of colour and a team of textures produce a wonderful medley of flavour! Make it in the morning, and enjoy it for supper.

Bacon slices, diced	6	6
Chopped onion	1 cup	250 mL
Garlic cloves, minced (or 1/2 tsp., 2 mL, powder)	2	2
Prepared chicken broth	5 cups	1.25 L
Can of white kidney beans (19 oz., 540 mL), rinsed and drained	1	1
Chopped yam (or sweet potato)	2 cups	500 mL
Sweet (or regular) chili sauce	2 tbsp.	30 mL
Pepper	1/2 tsp.	2 mL
Cooking oil	1 tsp.	5 mL
Chorizo sausages, casings removed, chopped	2	2
Fresh spinach, stems removed, lightly packed	3 cups	750 mL
Chopped fresh parsley (or 2 tsp., 10 mL, flakes)	3 tbsp.	45 mL
Lemon juice	1 tbsp.	15 mL

Cook bacon in a medium frying pan on medium until crisp. Remove to paper towels to drain. Remove and discard drippings, reserving 1 tbsp. (15 mL) in pan.

Add onion. Cook for 5 to 10 minutes, stirring often, until softened.

Add garlic and cook, stirring, for about 1 minute until fragrant. Transfer to your slow cooker. Stir in bacon and next 5 ingredients. Cook, covered, on Low for 8 to 10 hours or on High for 4 to 5 hours.

Heat cooking oil in same medium frying pan on medium. Add sausage and cook for 8 to 10 minutes, stirring occasionally, until no longer pink. Drain. Stir into bean mixture.

Add spinach and parsley. Stir well. Cook, covered, on High for about 15 minutes until spinach is wilted.

Stir in lemon juice. Makes about 9 cups (2.25 L).

1 cup (250 mL): 300 Calories; 14 g Total Fat (4 g Mono, 1.5 g Poly, 4.5 g Sat); 35 mg Cholesterol; 25 g Carbohydrate (6 g Fibre, 3 g Sugar); 17 g Protein; 850 mg Sodium

Pasta e Fagioli

Loaded with bacon, beans and pasta, this classic Italian soup is hearty and delicious. Serve with fresh crusty bread.

Bacon slices, diced	6	6
Chopped onion	1 cup	250 mL
Sliced carrot	1 cup	250 mL
Sliced celery	1 cup	250 mL
Garlic cloves, minced (or 1/2 tsp., 2 mL, powder)	2	2
Dried basil	1 tsp.	5 mL
Dried oregano	1 tsp.	5 mL
Pepper	1/2 tsp.	2 mL
Can of white kidney beans (19 oz., 540 mL), rinsed and drained	1	1
Can of diced tomatoes (28 oz., 796 mL), with juice	1	1
Prepared chicken broth	3 cups	750 mL
Water	1 cup	250 mL
Tomato paste (see Tip, page 38)	1/4 cup	60 mL
Bay leaves	2	2
Water	5 cups	1.25 L
Salt	1/2 tsp.	2 mL
Tubetti	1 cup	250 mL
Chopped fresh parsley	2 tbsp.	30 mL
Grated Parmesan cheese	1/4 cup	60 mL

Cook bacon in a medium frying pan on medium until crisp. Remove to paper towels to drain and discard all but 2 tsp. (10 mL) drippings. Transfer bacon to your slow cooker.

Heat remaining drippings in same frying pan on medium. Add next 7 ingredients. Cook for 5 to 10 minutes, stirring often, until onion is softened. Add to slow cooker.

Measure 1 cup (250 mL) beans onto a plate. Mash with a fork and add to slow cooker. Stir in next 5 ingredients and remaining beans. Cook, covered, on Low for 7 to 8 hours or on High for 3 1/2 to 4 hours. Discard bay leaves.

Combine water and salt in a large saucepan and bring to a boil. Add tubetti and boil, uncovered, for 10 to 12 minutes, stirring occasionally, until tender but firm. Drain. Add to slow cooker.

Stir in parsley. Sprinkle cheese on individual servings. Makes about 12 cups (3 L).

1 cup (250 mL): 180 Calories; 7 g Total Fat (3 g Mono, 1 g Poly, 2.5 g Sat); 15 mg Cholesterol; 19 g Carbohydrate (5 g Fibre, 2 g Sugar); 11 g Protein; 710 mg Sodium

Cock-a-Leekie

This soup comes straight from the Scottish Highlands to your slow cooker. The name may seem a bit nonsensical, but it's actually derived from the dish's traditional ingredients—rooster and leeks.

Bacon slices, diced	4	4
Sliced leek (white part only)	4 cups	1 L
Pearl barley	1/2 cup	125 mL
Chopped carrot	1 cup	250 mL
Chopped celery	1/2 cup	125 mL
Bone-in chicken parts, skin removed (see Note)	3 1/2 lbs.	1.6 kg
Prepared chicken broth	7 cups	1.75 L
Whole black peppercorns	8	8
Sprigs of fresh parsley	4	4
Sprig of fresh thyme	1	1
Bay leaf	1	1
Can of evaporated milk (3 3/4 oz., 110 mL)	1	1
All-purpose flour	1 tbsp.	15 mL

Cook bacon in a large frying pan on medium for about 5 minutes until almost crisp.

Add leek and cook for about 5 minutes, stirring occasionally, until leek starts to soften. Transfer to your slow cooker. Layer next 4 ingredients, in order given, over leek mixture. Pour broth over chicken.

Place next 4 ingredients on a 10 inch (25 cm) square piece of cheesecloth. Draw up corners and tie with string to form a bouquet garni. Submerge in liquid in slow cooker. Cook, covered, on Low for 8 to 10 hours or on High for 4 to 5 hours. Remove and discard bouquet garni. Transfer chicken to a cutting board using a slotted spoon. Remove chicken from bones. Cut chicken into bite-sized pieces and return to slow cooker. Discard bones.

Whisk evaporated milk into flour in a small bowl until smooth. Add to soup, stirring well. Cook, covered, on High for about 5 minutes until boiling and slightly thickened. Makes about 12 cups (3 L).

1 cup (250 mL): 310 Calories; 12 g Total Fat (5 g Mono, 3 g Poly, 4 g Sat); 90 mg Cholesterol; 16 g Carbohydrate (2 g Fibre, 2 g Sugar); 34 g Protein; 520 mg Sodium

Note: Use whichever cuts of chicken you prefer as long as the weight used is equal to that listed.

Manhattan Clam Chowder

Clam chowders are probably the best-known of all chowders, and they can be divided into two main types: Manhattan style and New England style. Both types have many ingredients in common, but the Manhattan style has a tomato base whereas the New England style has a cream base.

Cans of whole baby clams (5 oz., 142 g, each)	2	2
Water	6 cups	1.5 L
Cans of diced tomatoes (14 oz., 398 mL, each), with juice	2	2
Chopped onion	2 cups	500 mL
Chopped unpeeled red potato	2 cups	500 mL
Diced celery	1 cup	250 mL
Can of tomato paste (5 1/2 oz., 156 mL)	1	1
Diced carrot	1/2 cup	125 mL
Bacon slices, cooked crisp and crumbled	5	5
Dried thyme	1 tsp.	5 mL
Cayenne pepper	1/4 tsp.	1 mL

Drain liquid from clams into your slow cooker. Transfer clams to a small bowl. Chill, covered.

Add next 10 ingredients to slow cooker and stir. Cook, covered, on Low for 8 to 10 hours or on High for 4 to 5 hours. Stir in clams. Cook, covered, on High for about 10 minutes until heated through. Makes about 14 cups (3.5 L).

1 cup (250 mL): 130 Calories; 7 g Total Fat (4.5 g Mono, 1.5 g Poly, 3.5 g Sat); 15 mg Cholesterol; 14 g Carbohydrate (3 g Fibre, 3 g Sugar); 6 g Protein; 200 mg Sodium

Fall Bounty Soup

Vegetables aplenty decorate this thick, hearty soup, which is topped with French bread that has been covered in Gouda cheese and baked until golden.

Prepared vegetable broth	4 cups	1 L
Diced sweet potato (or yam)	2 cups	500 mL
Chopped cauliflower	2 cups	500 mL
Diced peeled potato	1 cup	250 mL
Chopped carrot	1 cup	250 mL
Chopped onion	1 cup	250 mL
Bay leaf	1	1
Granulated sugar	1 tsp.	5 mL
Dried thyme	1/2 tsp.	2 mL
Salt	1/2 tsp.	2 mL
Pepper	1/2 tsp.	2 mL
French bread slices, 1/2 inch (12 mm) thick	6	6
Grated Gouda cheese	1 cup	250 mL

Combine first 11 ingredients in your slow cooker. Cook, covered, on Low for 8 to 10 hours or on High for 4 to 5 hours. Remove and discard bay leaf.

Arrange bread slices on an ungreased baking sheet. Sprinkle each with 2 1/2 tbsp. (37 mL) cheese. Broil 4 inches (10 cm) from heat in oven for 2 to 3 minutes until cheese is melted and golden. Divide and ladle soup into 6 individual bowls. Top each with 1 bread slice. Makes 6 servings.

1 serving: 300 Calories; 8 g Total Fat (2.5 g Mono, 0.5 g Poly, 4.5 g Sat); 25 mg Cholesterol; 47 g Carbohydrate (5 g Fibre, 12 g Sugar); 12 g Protein; 1240 mg Sodium

Zesty Southwestern Soup

Turn up the heat with a steaming bowl of this spicy soup. Serve with tortilla chips instead of crackers.

Prepared vegetable broth	5 cups	1.25 L
Diced peeled potato	2 2/3 cups	650 mL
Thinly sliced onion	1 3/4 cups	425 mL
Thinly sliced celery	1 cup	250 mL
Can of diced green chillies (4 oz., 113 g), with juice	1	1
Roma (plum) tomatoes, seeds removed, chopped	2	2
Garlic cloves, minced (or 1/2 tsp., 2 mL, powder)	2	2
Chili powder	1 tsp.	5 mL
Ground cumin	1 tsp.	5 mL
Cayenne pepper	1/2 tsp.	2 mL
Grated sharp Cheddar cheese	1 cup	250 mL

Medium salsa, for garnish
Chopped fresh cilantro or parsley
   (or 3/4 tsp., 4 mL, dried), for garnish

Combine first 10 ingredients in your slow cooker. Cook, covered, on Low for 8 to 10 hours or on High for 4 to 5 hours. Carefully process with a hand blender or in a blender until smooth, following manufacturer's instructions for processing hot liquids.

Add cheese and stir until cheese is melted.

Garnish individual servings with salsa and cilantro. Makes about 6 1/2 cups (1.6 L).

1 cup (250 mL): 180 Calories; 7 g Total Fat (2 g Mono, 0 g Poly, 4.5 g Sat); 25 mg Cholesterol; 21 g Carbohydrate (3 g Fibre, 5 g Sugar); 8 g Protein; 990 mg Sodium

White Bean Borscht

This creamy beet and bean soup has a lovely touch of lemon and dill. Sour cream and fresh parsley garnishes are a nice touch.

Dried navy beans, rinsed and drained	1 cup	250 mL
Prepared chicken (or vegetable) broth	8 cups	2 L
Fresh medium beets, peeled, cut into 1/2 inch (12 mm) pieces	3	3
Finely chopped onion	1 cup	250 mL
Diced carrot	2/3 cup	150 mL
Finely chopped brown (or white) mushrooms	1/2 cup	125 mL
Garlic clove, minced (or 1/4 tsp., 1 mL, powder), optional	1	1
Bay leaf	1	1
Half-and-half cream	1/2 cup	125 mL
All-purpose flour	2 tbsp.	30 mL
Lemon juice	1 tbsp.	15 mL
Dill weed	1 tsp.	5 mL
Salt	1 tsp.	5 mL
Pepper	1/2 tsp.	2 mL
Sour cream (or half-and-half cream), for garnish		
Chopped fresh parsley, for garnish		

Measure beans into a medium bowl and add boiling water until 2 inches (5 cm) above beans. Let stand, covered, for at least 1 hour until cool. Drain. Rinse beans. Drain well and transfer to your slow cooker.

Stir in next 7 ingredients. Cook, covered, on Low for 9 to 12 hours or on High for 4 1/2 to 6 hours. Remove and discard bay leaf.

Stir cream into flour in a small bowl until smooth. Add to bean mixture, stirring well. Cook, covered, on High for about 15 minutes until boiling and slightly thickened.

Add next 4 ingredients. Stir well.

Garnish individual servings with sour cream and parsley. Makes about 9 3/4 cups (2.4 L).

1 cup (250 mL): 140 Calories; 2 g Total Fat (0 g Mono, 0 g Poly, 1 g Sat); 5 mg Cholesterol; 22 g Carbohydrate (5 g Fibre, 4 g Sugar); 9 g Protein; 760 mg Sodium

Polynesian Steak Strips

These tender strips of beef have a ginger soy sauce flavor. Serve on a bed of steaming basmati or coconut rice.

Beef steak, cut across the grain into thin slices	2 lbs.	900 g
Water	1/2 cup	125 mL
Ketchup	2 tbsp.	30 mL
Oyster sauce	1 tbsp.	15 mL
Soy sauce	1/4 cup	60 mL
Ground ginger	1/2 tsp.	2 mL
Garlic powder	1/4 tsp.	1 mL
Granulated sugar	1 tsp.	5 mL
Salt	1 tsp.	5 mL
Pepper	1/4 tsp.	1 mL

Place steak strips in your slow cooker.

Mix remaining 9 ingredients in a small bowl. Pour over strips and stir until meat is well coated. Cook, covered, on Low for 8 to 10 hours or on High for 4 to 5 hours. Makes 6 servings.

1 serving: 490 Calories; 33 g Total Fat (14 g Mono, 1 g Poly, 13 g Sat); 125 mg Cholesterol; 4 g Carbohydrate (0 g Fibre, 2 g Sugar); 42 g Protein; 1240 mg Sodium

Chinese Pepper Steak

A wok? Who needs it? You can serve up some great Asian flavours right in your slow cooker. Serve this fresh-tasting delight over aromatic basmati rice.

Large onion, thinly sliced	1	1
Cooking oil	1 tbsp.	15 mL
Beef inside round steak, cut into strips	2 lbs.	900 g
Can of diced tomatoes (14 oz., 398 mL), with juice	1	1
Soy sauce	1/4 cup	60 mL
Garlic clove, minced (or 1/2 tsp., 2 mL, powder)	2	2
Onion powder	1/2 tsp.	2 mL
Dried basil	1/4 tsp.	1 mL
Granulated sugar	1 tsp.	5 mL
Salt	1 tsp.	5 mL
Pepper	1/4 tsp.	1 mL
Paprika	1/4 tsp.	1 mL
Fresh bean sprouts	1 1/2 cups	375 mL
Snow peas, trimmed	1 1/2 cups	375 mL
Medium green pepper, thinly sliced	1	1
Medium red pepper, thinly sliced	1	1
Water	3 tbsp.	45 mL
Cornstarch	2 tbsp.	30 mL

Put onion into your slow cooker.

Heat a large frying pan on medium-high until very hot. Add cooking oil. Add beef and stir-fry for about 5 minutes until browned. Add to slow cooker.

Combine next 7 ingredients in a medium bowl. Pour over beef. Cook, covered, on Low for 6 to 7 hours or on High for 3 to 3 1/2 hours.

Stir in next 4 ingredients.

Stir water into cornstarch in a small cup. Add to slow cooker and stir well. Cook, covered, on High for about 15 minutes until liquid is slightly thickened and vegetables are tender-crisp. Makes about 9 cups (2.25 L).

1 cup (250 mL): 350 Calories; 21 g Total Fat (9 g Mono, 1.5 g Poly, 8 g Sat); 60 mg Cholesterol; 12 g Carbohydrate (2 g Fibre, 6 g Sugar); 27 g Protein; 860 mg Sodium

Shredded Beef on a Bun

The perfect meal for a casual crowd. Serve with coleslaw, potato salad and a variety of pickles, and let the party begin!

Sliced onion	1 cup	250 mL
Prepared chicken broth	1 cup	250 mL
Red wine vinegar	1/2 cup	125 mL
Brown sugar, packed	1/2 cup	125 mL
Tomato paste (see Tip, below)	1/4 cup	60 mL
Soy sauce	2 tbsp.	30 mL
Prepared mustard	2 tbsp.	30 mL
Garlic cloves, minced (or 1 tsp., 5 mL, powder)	4	4
Salt	1/2 tsp.	2 mL
Boneless blade (or chuck) roast	3 lbs.	1.4 kg
Kaiser rolls, split	12	12

Combine first 9 ingredients in your slow cooker.

Add roast and turn until coated. Cook, covered, on Low for 8 to 10 hours or on High for 4 to 5 hours. Transfer roast to a large plate. Cover to keep warm. Skim and discard any fat from surface of liquid in slow cooker. Strain liquid through a sieve into a large frying pan. Transfer solids to a small bowl and set aside. Bring liquid to a boil on medium-high. Boil gently for about 15 minutes, stirring occasionally, until sauce is thickened and reduced by almost half. Shred beef with 2 forks. Add to sauce. Add reserved solids and stir well.

Divide and spoon beef mixture onto bottom half of each roll. Cover each with top half of roll. Makes 12 beef buns.

1 beef bun: 550 Calories; 23 g Total Fat (10 g Mono, 2 g Poly, 9 g Sat); 100 mg Cholesterol; 43 g Carbohydrate (2 g Fibre, 9 g Sugar); 40 g Protein; 690 mg Sodium

Tip: If a recipe calls for less than an entire can of tomato paste, freeze the unopened can for 30 minutes. Open both ends and push the contents through one end. Slice off only what you need and freeze the remaining paste in a resealable freezer bag or plastic wrap for future use.

Beef in Red Wine

Get all your wining and dining done with one fantastic and rather fancy-tasting dish. Great served with noodles or mashed potatoes.

All-purpose flour	3 tbsp.	45 mL
Salt, to taste		
Stewing beef, cut into 1 1/2 inch (3.8 cm) cubes	1 lb.	454 g
Cooking oil	2 tsp.	10 mL
Thinly sliced onion	2 cups	500 mL
Thinly sliced carrot	1 cup	250 mL
Dry (or alcohol-free) red wine	1 cup	250 mL
Garlic cloves, minced (or 1/2 tsp., 2 mL, powder)	2	2
Pepper	1/4 tsp.	1 mL
Bay leaves	2	2
Sprig of fresh rosemary (or thyme)	1	1
Frozen peas	1/2 cup	125 mL

Combine flour and salt in a large resealable freezer bag. Add beef. Seal bag and toss until beef is coated.

Heat cooking oil in a large frying pan on medium-high. Add beef, discarding any remaining flour mixture. Cook for about 5 minutes, stirring occasionally, until browned. Transfer to your slow cooker.

Layer onion and carrot, in order given, over beef.

Combine next 3 ingredients in a small bowl. Pour over carrot. Add bay leaves and rosemary sprig. Cook, covered, on Low for 6 to 8 hours or on High for 3 to 4 hours. Stir in peas. Cook, covered, on High for about 5 minutes. Discard bay leaves and rosemary sprig. Makes about 4 cups (1 L).

1 cup (250 mL): 340 Calories; 12 g Total Fat (6 g Mono, 1 g Poly, 4 g Sat); 65 mg Cholesterol; 20 g Carbohydrate (3 g Fibre, 6 g Sugar); 26 g Protein; 115 mg Sodium

Beef Stew Diane

A less peppery cousin of Hungarian goulash, with a unique brandy accent. Serve over egg noodles with a salad on the side.

All-purpose flour	3 tbsp.	45 mL
Pepper	1/2 tsp.	2 mL
Beef stew meat	2 lbs.	900 g
Cooking oil	2 tbsp.	30 mL
Cooking oil	2 tsp.	10 mL
Chopped onion	1 1/2 cups	375 mL
Can of diced tomatoes (14 oz., 398 mL), with juice	1	1
Prepared beef broth	1 cup	250 mL
Worcestershire sauce	2 tbsp.	30 mL
Sour cream	1/4 cup	60 mL
Brandy (or apple juice)	2 1/2 tbsp.	37 mL
Chopped fresh parsley (or 1 1/2 tsp., 7 mL, dried)	2 tbsp.	30 mL

Combine flour and pepper in a large resealable freezer bag. Add 1/2 of beef. Seal bag and toss until beef is coated. Repeat with remaining beef. Heat first amount of cooking oil in a large frying pan on medium. Add beef in 2 batches. Cook for 5 to 10 minutes per batch, stirring occasionally, until browned. Transfer to your slow cooker.

Heat second amount of cooking oil in same large frying pan on medium. Add onion and cook for 5 to 10 minutes, stirring often, until softened. Stir into beef.

Add next 3 ingredients to beef mixture. Stir well. Cook, covered, on Low for 8 to 9 hours or on High for 4 to 4 1/2 hours.

Add remaining 3 ingredients. Stir well. Makes 8 servings.

1 serving: 280 Calories; 16 g Total Fat (7 g Mono, 2 g Poly, 4.5 g Sat); 65 mg Cholesterol; 8 g Carbohydrate (1 g Fibre, 3 g Sugar); 26 g Protein; 290 mg Sodium

Beef Brisket

Brisket is a one of the tougher cuts of beef, but the long, slow cooking process makes this dish tender and delicious. The leftover meat makes great sandwiches.

Medium carrots, cut into thin slices	6	6
Boneless beef brisket, trimmed of fat	4 1/2 lbs.	2 kg
Red (or alcohol-free) wine	1/2 cup	125 mL
Prepared beef broth	1/2 cup	125 mL
Onion powder	1/2 tsp.	2 mL
Ground rosemary	1/4 tsp.	1 mL
Pepper	1/4 tsp.	1 mL

Place carrot into your slow cooker. Lay brisket over top. If your cooker is too small, cut brisket in half.

Combine 5 remaining ingredients in a small bowl. Pour over brisket. Cook, covered, on Low for 10 to 12 hours or on High for 5 to 6 hours until very tender. Makes 12 servings.

1 serving: 540 Calories; 44 g Total Fat (20 g Mono, 1.5 g Poly, 18 g Sat); 100 mg Cholesterol; 3 g Carbohydrate (1 g Fibre, 1 g Sugar); 29 g Protein; 170 mg Sodium

Tasty Mex Casserole

Loaded with beef, corn and macaroni, this casserole is sure to please the whole family. To control the amount of heat in this dish, adjust the amount of green chilies and chilli powder to suit your taste.

Lean ground beef	1 1/2 lbs.	680 g
White vinegar	3 tbsp.	45 mL
Chili powder	1 tbsp.	15 mL
Dried whole oregano	1 tsp.	5 mL
Garlic powder	1/4 tsp.	1 mL
Salt	1 1/2 tsp.	7 mL
Pepper	1/4 tsp.	1 mL
Chopped onion	1 1/2 cups	375 mL
Medium green pepper, chopped	1	1
Can of chopped green chilies (4 oz., 114 mL), drained	1	1
Canned kernel corn (12 oz., 341 mL), drained	1	1
Elbow macaroni, partially cooked, drained and rinsed	1 cup	250 mL
Canned tomatoes (14 oz., 398 mL), with juice, broken up	2	2
Chili powder	2 tsp.	10 mL
Parsley flakes	1 tsp.	5 mL
Dried whole oregano	1/2 tsp.	2 mL
Granulated sugar	2 tsp.	10 mL
Salt	1/2 tsp.	2 mL
Pepper	1/4 tsp.	1 mL
Grated Monterey Jack cheese, for garnish		

Mix first 7 ingredients in a large bowl. Scramble-fry in a non-stick frying pan over medium heat until browned. Drain.

Combine onion, green pepper, green chilies, corn and partially cooked macaroni in your slow cooker. Stir in beef mixture.

Combine remaining 7 ingredients in a medium bowl. Stir well. Pour over beef mixture. Stir. Cook, covered, on Low for 8 hours or on High for 4 hours. Sprinkle individual servings with cheese. Makes 10 cups (2.5 L).

1 cup (250 mL): 240 Calories; 10 g Total Fat (4.5 g Mono, 0 g Poly, 4 g Sat); 40 mg Cholesterol; 18 g Carbohydrate (3 g Fibre, 7 g Sugar); 16 g Protein; 710 mg Sodium

Beef and Lentils

Tangy tomato and barbecue flavours add some zip to ground beef and lentils. This dish can be served on its own or over rice.

Can of diced tomatoes (28 oz., 796 mL), with juice	1	1
Can of lentils (19 oz., 540 mL), rinsed and drained	1	1
Finely chopped onion	1 1/2 cups	375 mL
Finely chopped celery	1/2 cup	125 mL
Barbecue sauce	3 tbsp.	45 mL
Sweet (or regular) chilli sauce	2 1/2 tbsp.	37 mL
Balsamic vinegar	1 tbsp.	15 mL
Bay leaf	1	1
Salt	1/4 tsp.	1 mL
Pepper	1/8 tsp.	0.5 mL
Cooking oil	2 tsp.	10 mL
Lean ground beef	1 lb.	454 g
All-purpose flour	1 1/2 tbsp.	22 mL
Prepared beef broth	1/4 cup	60 mL
Finely chopped fresh parsley (or 2 tsp., 10 mL, flakes), optional	3 tbsp.	45 mL

Combine first 10 ingredients in your slow cooker.

Heat cooking oil in a large frying pan on medium. Add ground beef and scramble-fry for 5 to 10 minutes until no longer pink. Drain.

Sprinkle flour over beef. Heat, stirring, on medium for 1 minute. Slowly add broth, stirring constantly and scraping any brown bits from bottom of pan. Add to tomato mixture. Stir well. Cook, covered, on Low for 8 to 10 hours or on High for 4 to 5 hours. Remove and discard bay leaf.

Add parsley. Stir well. Makes 6 servings.

1 serving: 380 Calories; 15 g Total Fat (7 g Mono, 1.5 g Poly, 4.5 g Sat); 50 mg Cholesterol; 35 g Carbohydrate (6 g Fibre, 11 g Sugar); 28 g Protein; 540 mg Sodium

Lasagna

This dish tastes just like lasagna, but it doesn't have the layers. Serve with garlic bread and a fresh garden salad.

Lean ground beef	1 1/2 lbs.	680 g
Finely chopped onion	3/4 cup	175 mL
Canned tomatoes (14 oz., 398 mL), with juice, broken up	2	2
Can of tomato paste (5 1/2 oz., 156 mL)	1	1
Creamed cottage cheese	1 cup	250 mL
Grated mozzarella cheese	2 cups	500 mL
Granulated sugar	2 tsp.	10 mL
Parsley flakes	1 tsp.	5 mL
Dried whole oregano	1/2 tsp.	2 mL
Garlic powder	1/4 tsp.	1 mL
Dried sweet basil	1/4 tsp.	1 mL
Salt	1 1/4 tsp.	6 mL
Pepper	1/2 tsp.	2 mL
Oven-ready lasagna noodles, broken into bite-size pieces	8	8

Scramble-fry ground beef in a non-stick frying pan until browned. Drain well. Turn into your slow cooker.

Add remaining 12 ingredients, stirring well. Stir in lasagne noodle pieces. Cook, covered, on Low for 7 to 9 hours or on High for 3 1/2 to 4 1/2 hours. Makes 10 cups (2.5 L).

1 cup (250 mL): 390 Calories; 17 g Total Fat (7 g Mono, 1 g Poly, 7 g Sat); 65 mg Cholesterol; 29 g Carbohydrate (5 g Fibre, 4 g Sugar); 30 g Protein; 1100 mg Sodium

Curried Beef

Serve this curry over hot basmati rice with fresh naan on the side to scoop up the fragrant sauce. Delicious!

Beef stew meat, cut into 1 1/2 inch (3.8 cm) thick cubes or strips	2 lbs.	900 g
Medium onions, cut into small chunks	2	2
All-purpose flour	3 tbsp.	45 mL
Salt	1 1/2 tsp.	7 mL
Pepper	3/4 tsp.	4 mL
Garlic cloves, minced	2	2
Onion powder	1/2 tsp.	2 mL
Paprika	1/2 tsp.	2 mL
Dried basil	1/2 tsp.	2 mL
Curry powder	1 1/2 tsp.	7 mL
Can of tomato sauce (7.5 oz., 213 mL, each)	2	2
Granulated sugar	1/2 tsp.	2 mL
Chopped fresh parsely or cilantro, for garnish		

Combine first 10 ingredients in your slow cooker. Stir well to coat beef, onion and garlic with flour and spices.

Stir remaining 3 ingredients in a small bowl. Pour over beef mixture. Cook, covered, on Low for 8 to 10 hours or on High for 4 to 5 hours. Garnish individual servings with parsely or cilantro. Makes 6 cups (1.5 L).

1 cup (250 mL): 300 Calories; 13 g Total Fat (6 g Mono, 0.5 g Poly, 5 g Sat); 85 mg Cholesterol; 10 g Carbohydrate (1 g Fibre, 4 g Sugar); 34 g Protein; 1120 mg Sodium

Mexi Wraps

Tender beef and beans in a thick chili pepper and tomato sauce. A family favourite.

Cooking oil	2 tbsp.	30 mL
Inside round steak, thinly sliced (see Tip, page 55)	2 lbs.	900 g
Water	2 tbsp.	30 mL
All-purpose flour	2 tbsp.	30 mL
Can of white kidney beans (19 oz., 540 mL) rinsed and drained	1	1
Can of diced tomatoes (14 oz., 398 mL), drained	1	1
Chopped onion	1 cup	250 mL
Chopped red or green pepper	1 cup	250 mL
Frozen kernel corn	1/2 cup	125 mL
Can of diced green chilies, drained (4 oz., 113 g)	1	1
Chopped fresh oregano leaves (or 1 1/2 tsp., 7 mL, dried)	2 tbsp.	30 mL
Tomato paste (see Tip, page 38)	2 tbsp.	30 mL
Chili powder	1 tbsp.	15 mL
Garlic cloves, minced (or 1/2 tsp., 2 mL, powder)	2	2
Ground cumin	1 tsp.	5 mL
Salt	1/4 tsp.	1 mL
Grated medium Cheddar cheese	1 cup	250 mL
Flour tortillas (9 inch, 23 cm, diameter)	10	10
Chopped or torn romaine lettuce, lightly packed	1 cup	250 mL

Heat cooking oil in a large frying pan on medium-high. Add beef in 2 batches. Cook for 3 to 4 minutes per batch, stirring occasionally, until browned. Transfer to your slow cooker.

Combine water and flour in a small cup, stirring until smooth. Pour over beef and stir.

Add next 12 ingredients and stir well. Cook, covered, on Low for 7 to 8 hours or on High for 3 1/2 to 4 hours.

Sprinkle 1 1/2 tbsp. (22 mL) cheese down centre of each tortilla. Spoon 1/2 cup (125 mL) beef mixture onto cheese. Divide and scatter lettuce over beef mixture. Fold bottom edge and sides of each tortilla over filling to enclose, leaving top open. Makes 10 wraps.

1 wrap: 420 Calories; 17 g Total Fat (7 g Mono, 2 g Poly, 6 g Sat); 45 mg Cholesterol; 37 g Carbohydrate (7 g Fibre, 3 g Sugar); 31 g Protein; 630 mg Sodium

Tip: To slice meat easily, place it in the freezer for about 30 minutes until it is just beginning to freeze. If you are using meat from a frozen state, partially thaw it before hand.

Slowpoke Cabbage Bake

A savoury mushroom meat sauce tops tender cabbage wedges in this simple but tasty dish.

Large head of savoy (or green) cabbage (about 1 3/4 lbs., 790 g), cut into 8 wedges	1	1
Bacon slices	6	6
Lean ground beef	1 lb.	454 g
Chopped onion	1/2 cup	125 mL
Garlic clove, minced (or 1/4 tsp., 1 mL, powder)	1	1
Can of condensed cream of mushroom soup (10 oz., 284 mL)	1	1
Can of mushroom stems and pieces (10 oz., 284 mL), with liquid	1	1
Prepared beef broth	1/2 cup	125 mL
Tomato paste (see Tip, page 38)	3 tbsp.	45 mL
Dried thyme	1/2 tsp.	2 mL
Dried whole oregano	1/4 tsp.	1 mL
Salt	1/2 tsp.	2 mL

Put cabbage wedges, rounded-side up, into your slow cooker.

Cook bacon in a large frying pan on medium until crisp. Remove to paper towels to drain. Crumble and set aside. Remove and discard drippings, reserving 1 tbsp. (15 mL) in pan.

Heat reserved drippings in same frying pan on medium. Add ground beef, onion and garlic. Scramble-fry for 5 to 10 minutes until beef is no longer pink. Drain.

Add bacon and remaining 7 ingredients. Stir well. Pour over cabbage. Do not stir. Cook, covered, on Low for 8 to 10 hours or on High for 4 to 5 hours. Makes 8 servings.

1 serving: 220 Calories; 13 g Total Fat (7 g Mono, 1.5 g Poly, 6 g Sat); 40 mg Cholesterol; 10 g Carbohydrate (3 g Fibre, 5 g Sugar); 15 g Protein; 470 mg Sodium

Rosemary Lamb

These hearty lamb shanks in a rustic red wine and rosemary sauce pair perfectly with homemade garlic mashed potatoes.

Coarsely chopped carrot	2 cups	500 mL
Thinly sliced onion	1 cup	250 mL
All-purpose flour	1/4 cup	60 mL
Salt	1/2 tsp.	2 mL
Pepper	1/2 tsp.	2 mL
Lamb shanks (3/4 lb., 340 g, each)	4	4
Cooking oil	1 tbsp.	15 mL
Dry red (or alcohol-free) wine	2/3 cup	150 mL
Tomato paste (see Tip, page 38)	2 tbsp.	30 mL
Chopped fresh rosemary leaves	1 1/2 tbsp.	25 mL
(or 1 1/4 tsp., 6 mL, dried, crushed)		

Put carrot and onion into your slow cooker.

Combine next 3 ingredients in a large resealable freezer bag. Add 1/2 of lamb shanks. Seal bag and toss until lamb is coated. Repeat with remaining lamb. Heat cooking oil in a large frying pan on medium-high. Add lamb in 2 batches, reserving any remaining flour mixture. Cook for 5 to 7 minutes per batch, turning occasionally, until browned. Arrange on top of vegetables. Sprinkle with remaining flour mixture.

Combine remaining 3 ingredients in a liquid measure or bowl. Pour over lamb. Cook, covered, on Low for 8 to 10 hours or on High for 4 to 5 hours. Transfer lamb to a large serving platter and cover to keep warm. Skim and discard any fat from surface of liquid in slow cooker. Drizzle liquid from slow cooker over individual servings. Makes 4 servings.

1 serving: 570 Calories; 18 g Total Fat (8 g Mono, 2.5 g Poly, 5 g Sat); 220 mg Cholesterol; 19 g Carbohydrate (3 g Fibre, 6 g Sugar); 72 g Protein; 500 mg Sodium

Lamb with Spinach

Vibrant green spinach and red, juicy tomatoes add wonderful colour to delicately seasoned lamb. Serve with couscous.

Cooking oil	1 tbsp.	15 mL
Lamb stew meat	2 lbs.	900 g
Sliced fresh white mushrooms	2 cups	500 mL
Chopped onion	1 cup	250 mL
Chopped red pepper	1 cup	250 mL
Can of diced tomatoes (14 oz., 398 mL) with juice	1	1
Prepared chicken broth	1 cup	250 mL
Chopped fresh thyme leaves (or 1/2 tsp., 2 mL, dried)	2 tsp.	10 mL
Granulated sugar	1/2 tsp.	2 mL
Salt	1/4 tsp.	1 mL
Pepper	1/4 tsp.	1 mL
Water	1 tbsp.	15 mL
Cornstarch	1 tbsp.	15 mL
Fresh spinach, stems removed, lightly packed	2 cups	500 mL
Chopped fresh basil (see Note)	2 tbsp.	30 mL

Heat cooking oil in a large frying pan on medium-high. Add lamb in 2 batches and cook for 8 to 10 minutes per batch, stirring occasionally, until browned. Transfer to your slow cooker.

Add mushrooms, onion and red pepper to same large frying pan. Cook on medium for 5 to 10 minutes, stirring often, until onion is softened. Add to lamb in slow cooker.

Combine next 6 ingredients in a medium bowl. Pour over lamb mixture, stirring well. Cook, covered, on Low for 8 to 10 hours or on High for 4 to 5 hours.

Combine water and cornstarch in a small cup, stirring until smooth. Add to lamb mixture and stir well. Cook, covered, on High for 5 to 10 minutes until sauce is thickened.

Stir in spinach and basil. Makes 8 servings.

1 serving: 310 Calories; 12 g Total Fat (5 g Mono, 1.5 g Poly, 3.5 g Sat); 120 mg Cholesterol; 9 g Carbohydrate (2 g Fibre, 2 g Sugar); 40 g Protein; 290 mg Sodium

Note: If you use dried basil instead of fresh, reduce the amount to 1 1/2 tsp. (7 mL) and add it to the tomato mixture before cooking.

Stuffed Pork Tenderloin

Although they are simple to prepare, these tenderloins are fancy enough to serve to company and are sure to impress your guests.

Fine dry bread crumbs	1 1/2 cups	375 mL
Cooked bacon slices, crumbled	3	3
Finely chopped celery	1/4 cup	60 mL
Finely chopped onion	1/4 cup	60 mL
Poultry seasoning	1/2 tsp.	2 mL
Parsley flakes	1/2 tsp.	2 mL
Salt	1/2 tsp.	2 mL
Pepper	1/4 tsp.	1 mL
Prepared chicken broth	2/3 cup	150 mL
Pork tenderloins (about 1 1/2 lbs., 680 g, total)	2	2

Mix first 7 ingredients in a bowl.

Pour broth over stuffing mixture. Toss, adding more water if needed to moisten.

Slice each tenderloin lengthwise about halfway through, careful not to cut through to other side. Press open to flatten. Pound with a mallet or rolling pin to an even thickness. Spread stuffing mixture on cut sides of tenderloins. Roll up from long side and tie with butcher's string or secure with metal skewers. Transfer to your slow cooker. Cook, covered, on Low for 6 to 7 hours. Makes 6 servings.

1 serving: 280 Calories; 8 g Total Fat (3.5 g Mono, 1 g Poly, 2.5 g Sat); 90 mg Cholesterol; 12 g Carbohydrate (1 g Fibre, 1 g Sugar); 37 g Protein; 510 mg Sodium

Ham Potato Bake

This recipe is a perfect example of a whole that is greater than the sum of its parts. Although it has only four simple ingredients, this dish has outstanding flavour. A festive favourite to be sure.

Small sweet potatoes, peeled, cut into bite-size pieces	2 1/2 lbs.	1.1 kg
Boneless ham steak	1 1/2 lbs.	680 g
Brown sugar, packed	1/3 cup	75 mL
Prepared mustard	1 tsp.	5 mL

Put sweet potato into your slow cooker. Place ham steak over top.

Mix brown sugar and mustard in a small cup. Sprinkle over ham. Cook, covered, on Low for 7 to 8 hours or on High for 3 1/2 to 4 hours. Cut ham into serving-size pieces. Makes 4 servings.

1 serving: 510 Calories; 6 g Total Fat (3 g Mono, 1 g Poly, 2 g Sat); 75 mg Cholesterol; 76 g Carbohydrate (9 g Fibre, 32 g Sugar); 36 g Protein; 1940 mg Sodium

ᘯ Many people confuse sweet potatoes with yams. While the two share some similarities, they come from different plants. Sweet potatoes are tubers of the morning glory plant native to Central America. Despite their name, they are not related to potatoes, and they are sweeter and less starchy than yams. The most commonly found variety in supermarkets has orange flesh and becomes soft and moist when cooked. Yams are tubers of a plant native to Africa and east Asia. They are starchier and earthier tasting than sweet potatoes; their flesh tends to be paler and has a drier, firmer texture when cooked.

Corny Shepherd's Pie

Tender polenta, a mixture of cornmeal and cheese, tops spicy sausage and tender vegetables in this slow cooker version of shepherd's pie.

Cooking oil	1 tsp.	5 mL
Hot Italian sausages, casings removed, chopped	1 lb.	454 g
Lean ground pork	1 lb.	454 g
Chopped onion	1/2 cup	125 mL
Chopped celery	1/2 cup	125 mL
Cans of diced tomatoes (14 oz., 398 mL, each), with juice	2	2
Frozen kernel corn	1 cup	250 mL
Dried whole oregano	1 tsp.	5 mL
Water	3 cups	750 mL
Butter (or hard margarine)	1 tbsp.	15 mL
Pepper	1/4 tsp.	1 mL
Yellow regular (or coarse) cornmeal	1 cup	250 mL
Grated Parmesan cheese	1/2 cup	125 mL
Parsley flakes	2 tsp.	10 mL

Heat cooking oil in a large frying pan on medium. Add next 4 ingredients and scramble-fry for 8 to 10 minutes until sausage and ground pork are no longer pink. Drain. Transfer to your slow cooker.

Add tomatoes, corn and oregano. Stir well.

For the topping, bring water to a boil on medium-high. Add butter and pepper. Reduce heat to low. Slowly add cornmeal, stirring constantly, until water is absorbed. Cook for 2 to 3 minutes, stirring occasionally, until mixture is very thick.

Add Parmesan cheese and parsley. Stir well. Spread evenly on top of sausage mixture. Cook, covered, on Low for 8 to 9 hours or on High for 4 to 4 1/2 hours. Makes 8 servings.

1 serving: 369 Calories; 22 g Total Fat (8 g Mono, 2 g Poly, 8 g Sat); 50 mg Cholesterol; 25 g Carbohydrate (2 g Fibre, 3 g Sugar); 18 g Protein; 890 mg Sodium

Savoury Side Ribs

As a seasoning for ribs, one generally thinks of garlic or ginger, but the allspice and cinnamon in these saucy ribs really makes them stand out of the crowd.

Garlic powder	1 tsp.	5 mL
Ground ginger	1 tsp.	5 mL
Dry mustard	1 tsp.	5 mL
Onion powder	1 tsp.	5 mL
Cayenne pepper	1/2 tsp.	2 mL
Ground allspice	1/4 tsp.	1 mL
Ground cinnamon	1/4 tsp.	1 mL
Pork side ribs, trimmed of fat and cut into 3-bone portions	3 1/2 lbs.	1.6 kg
Large onion, thinly sliced	1	1
Barbecue sauce	1 cup	250 mL
Water	1/2 cup	125 mL
Chili sauce	1/3 cup	75 mL

Combine first 7 ingredients in a small cup. Divide and sprinkle over both sides of each rib portion. Layer ribs alternately with onion slices in your slow cooker.

Combine barbecue sauce, water and chili sauce in a small bowl. Pour over ribs. Do not stir. Cook, covered, on Low for 8 to 10 hours or on High for 4 to 5 hours. Remove ribs with a slotted spoon to a large serving platter. Skim and discard any fat from surface of liquid in slow cooker. Serve with ribs. Makes 8 servings.

1 serving: 540 Calories; 36 g Total Fat (16 g Mono, 3.5 g Poly, 14 g Sat); 140 mg Cholesterol; 15 g Carbohydrate (0 g Fibre, 3 g Sugar); 38 g Protein; 730 mg Sodium

Pork and Mushroom Ragout

A white wine and tomato cream sauce coats tender pork and mushrooms in this dish that is simple to prepare but has sophisticated flavour. Serve over egg noodles.

All-purpose flour	3 tbsp.	45 mL
Boneless pork shoulder butt roast or steaks, trimmed of fat and cut into 3/4 inch (2 cm) pieces	2 lbs.	900 g
Cooking oil	1 tbsp.	15 mL
Cooking oil	1 tbsp.	15 mL
Sliced fresh white mushrooms	2 1/2 cups	625 mL
Large leek (white part only), thinly sliced	1	1
Prepared chicken broth	1 1/4 cups	300 mL
Dry white (or alcohol-free) wine	1 cup	250 mL
Tomato paste (see Tip, page 38)	2 tbsp.	30 mL
Salt	1/4 tsp.	1 mL
Pepper	1/2 tsp.	2 mL
Sour cream	1/4 cup	60 mL

Measure flour into a large resealable freezer bag. Add 1/2 of pork. Seal bag and toss until pork is coated. Repeat with remaining pork. Heat first amount of cooking oil in a large frying pan on medium-high. Add pork in 2 batches. Cook for 8 to 10 minutes per batch, stirring occasionally, until browned. Transfer to your slow cooker.

Heat second amount of cooking oil in same large frying pan on medium. Add mushrooms and leek. Cook for about 5 minutes, stirring often, until leek is softened.

Slowly add broth, stirring constantly and scraping any brown bits from bottom of pan. Add next 4 ingredients. Heat, stirring, for about 2 minutes until boiling. Pour over pork. Do not stir. Cook, covered, on Low for 8 to 10 hours or on High for 4 to 5 hours.

Add sour cream. Stir well. Makes 8 servings.

1 serving: 268 Calories; 13 g Total Fat (6 g Mono, 2 g Poly, 4 g Sat); 75 mg Cholesterol; 7 g Carbohydrate (1 g Fibre, 2 g Sugar); 25 g Protein; 246 mg Sodium

Jamaican Pork and Couscous

Mildly spiced chops served with a sweet couscous blend. Both components are made separately in the slow cooker. The couscous cooks up quickly and dinner is ready!

Brown sugar, packed	1 tsp.	5 mL
Dried thyme	1/2 tsp.	2 mL
Ground allspice	1/2 tsp.	2 mL
Ground ginger	1/2 tsp.	2 mL
Cayenne pepper	1/4 tsp.	2 mL
Ground cinnamon	1/4 tsp.	2 mL
Salt	1/4 tsp.	2 mL
Pepper	1/4 tsp.	2 mL
Bone-in pork chops, trimmed of fat	8	8
Canola oil	2 tsp.	10 mL
Chopped onion	1 1/2 cups	375 mL
Chopped peeled orange-fleshed sweet potato	1 1/2 cups	375 mL
Unsweetened applesauce	1 cup	250 mL
Prepared chicken broth	3/4 cup	175 mL
Frozen peas, thawed	1 cup	250 mL
Whole wheat couscous	1 cup	250 mL
Lime juice	1 tbsp.	15 mL

Combine first 8 ingredients in a small cup. Rub over both sides of pork chops.

Heat canola oil in a large frying pan on medium-high. Cook pork chops, in 2 batches, for about 1 minute per side, until browned. Transfer to a large plate.

Combine next 4 ingredients in your slow cooker. Arrange pork chops over top. Do not stir. Place a double layer of tea towels over slow cooker liner and cover with lid. Cook on Low for 5 to 6 hours or on High for 2 1/2 to 3 hours. Transfer pork chops to a large serving plate and cover to keep warm. Skim and discard fat from cooking liquid.

Add remaining 3 ingredients to slow cooker and stir. Cook, covered, on High for about 10 minutes until liquid is absorbed and couscous is tender. Serve with pork chops. Makes 8 servings.

1 serving: 370 Calories; 16 g Total Fat (7 g Mono, 2 g Poly, 5 g Sat); 60 mg Cholesterol; 33 g Carbohydrate (4 g Fibre, 8 g Sugar); 25 g Protein; 130 mg Sodium

Sweet and Sour Pork

Tender pork in a sweet sauce accented with pineapple, green pepper and carrot. Serve over rice or your favourite noodles.

Chopped onion	1 cup	250 mL
Diced carrot	1 cup	250 mL
Apple cider vinegar	1/4 cup	60 mL
Brown sugar, packed	1/4 cup	60 mL
Soy sauce	2 tbsp.	30 mL
Ketchup	2 tbsp.	30 mL
Garlic cloves, minced (or 1/2 tsp., 2 mL, powder)	2	2
Ground ginger	1 tsp.	5 mL
Pork stew meat	2 lbs.	900 g
Water	2 tbsp.	30 mL
Cornstarch	2 tbsp.	30 mL
Can of pineapple tidbits (14 oz., 398 mL), with juice	1	1
Sliced green pepper	1 cup	250 mL
Sliced red pepper	1 cup	250 mL

Combine first 9 ingredients in your slow cooker. Cook, covered, on Low for 8 to 9 hours or on High for 4 to 4 1/2 hours.

Combine water and cornstarch in a small cup, stirring until smooth. Pour over pork mixture and stir. Add pineapple and green pepper. Stir well. Cook, covered, on High for about 15 minutes until green pepper is tender-crisp and sauce is thickened. Makes 8 servings.

1 serving: 370 Calories; 21 g Total Fat (9 g Mono, 2.5 g Poly, 7 g Sat); 67 mg Cholesterol; 22 g Carbohydrate (1 g Fibre, 17 g Sugar); 22 g Protein; 364 mg Sodium

Mint and Cider Pork

Beautiful pearl onions and colourful baby carrots surround tender pork that is seasoned with sweet apple cider and a hint of mint.

All-purpose flour	3 tbsp.	45 mL
Boneless pork shoulder butt roast or steaks, trimmed of fat and cut into 3/4 inch (2 cm) pieces	2 lbs.	900 g
Cooking oil	1 tbsp.	15 mL
Baby carrots	1 lb.	454 g
Tiny white pearl onions, skins removed	2 cups	500 mL
Apple cider	1 cup	250 mL
Prepared beef broth	2/3 cup	150 mL
Salt	1/4 tsp.	1 mL
Pepper	1/4 tsp.	1 mL
Frozen peas	1 cup	250 mL
Chopped fresh mint leaves (or 1 tbsp., 15 mL, dried)	1/4 cup	60 mL

Measure flour into a large resealable freezer bag. Add 1/2 of pork. Seal bag and toss until pork is coated. Repeat with remaining pork. Heat cooking oil in a large frying pan on medium-high. Cook pork in 2 batches for 8 to 10 minutes per batch, stirring occasionally, until browned. Transfer to your slow cooker.

Stir in next 6 ingredients. Cook, covered, on Low for 8 to 10 hours or on High for 4 to 5 hours.

Add peas and mint. Stir well. Cook, covered, on High for about 10 minutes until peas are heated through. Makes 8 servings.

1 serving: 258 Calories; 9 g Total Fat (4.5 g Mono, 1.5 g Poly, 3 g Sat); 71 mg Cholesterol; 16 g Carbohydrate (3 g Fibre, 9 g Sugar); 26 g Protein; 291 mg Sodium

Currant Thyme Pork

This dish smells amazing as it cooks; it will have everyone rushing to the kitchen to see what's for dinner.

Chopped onion	3/4 cup	175 mL
Chopped carrot	1 1/2 cups	375 mL
Chopped parsnip	1/2 cup	125 mL
Baby potatoes, larger ones cut in half	2 lbs.	900 g
All-purpose flour	3 tbsp.	45 mL
Boneless pork shoulder butt roast, trimmed of fat and cut into 3/4 inch (2 cm) pieces	2 lbs.	900 g
Cooking oil	1 tbsp.	15 mL
Sprigs of fresh thyme	2	2
Prepared chicken broth	1 1/2 cups	375 mL
Redcurrant jelly	1/3 cup	75 mL
Garlic cloves	6	6
Salt	1/4 tsp.	1 mL
Pepper	1/2 tsp.	2 mL

Layer first 4 ingredients, in order given, in your slow cooker.

Measure flour into a large resealable freezer bag. Add 1/2 of pork. Seal bag and toss until pork is coated. Repeat with remaining pork. Heat cooking oil in a large frying pan on medium-high. Cook pork in 2 batches for 8 to 10 minutes per batch, stirring occasionally, until browned. Scatter evenly on top of potatoes. Place thyme sprigs on top of pork.

Combine next 5 ingredients in a small bowl. Pour over pork. Do not stir. Cook, covered, on Low for 8 to 10 hours or on High for 4 to 5 hours. Remove and discard thyme sprigs. Makes 8 servings.

1 serving: 352 Calories; 9 g Total Fat (4.5 g Mono, 1.5 g Poly, 3 g Sat); 71 mg Cholesterol; 38 g Carbohydrate (3 g Fibre, 8 g Sugar); 28 g Protein; 273 mg Sodium

Crock of Herbed Pork

Tender, savoury pork is seasoned with basil, oregano and a dash of sherry. Serve with roasted garlic potatoes and Brussels sprouts.

All-purpose flour	2 tbsp.	30 mL
Boneless pork shoulder butt roast or steaks, trimmed of fat and cut into 3/4 inch (2 cm) pieces	1 1/2 lbs.	680 g
Bacon slices, diced	8	8
Chopped carrot	1 cup	250 mL
Chopped onion	1 cup	250 mL
Prepared chicken broth	1 cup	250 mL
Dry sherry (or chicken broth)	1/3 cup	75 mL
Chopped fresh oregano leaves (or 3/4 tsp., 4 mL, dried)	1 tbsp.	15 mL
Salt	1/4 tsp.	1 mL
Pepper	1/2 tsp.	2 mL
Chopped flat leaf parsley (see Note)	2 tbsp.	30 mL

Measure flour into a large resealable freezer bag. Add pork. Seal bag and toss until pork is coated. Set aside.

Cook bacon in a large frying pan on medium until crisp. Remove to paper towels to drain. Set aside. Remove and discard drippings, reserving 1 tbsp. (15 mL) in pan. Heat reserved drippings in same frying pan on medium-high. Add pork and cook for 8 to 10 minutes, stirring occasionally, until browned. Transfer to your slow cooker.

Add bacon and next 7 ingredients. Stir well. Cook, covered, on Low for 8 to 10 hours or on High for 4 to 5 hours.

Add basil and stir well. Makes 6 servings.

1 serving: 450 Calories; 30 g Total Fat (14 g Mono, 3.5 g Poly, 10 g Sat); 106 mg Cholesterol; 8 g Carbohydrate (1 g Fibre, 3 g Sugar); 31 g Protein; 709 mg Sodium

Note: If you use dried parsley instead of fresh, reduce the amount to 1 1/2 tsp. (7 mL) and add it to the carrot mixture before cooking.

Snappy Pineapple Chicken

The chicken and sweet bites of pineapple get a lively snap from ginger, lemon pepper and chili sauce. Serve over jasmine or coconut rice.

Large onion, cut into 8 wedges	1	1
Baby carrots	12 oz.	340 g
All-purpose flour	1/4 cup	60 mL
Paprika	2 1/2 tsp.	12 mL
Lemon pepper	2 1/2 tsp.	12 mL
Ground ginger	2 1/2 tsp.	12 mL
Boneless, skinless chicken breast halves (about 5 oz., 140 g, each), each cut into 2 pieces	6	6
Boneless, skinless chicken thighs (about 3 oz., 85 g, each)	12	12
Prepared chicken broth	1 cup	250 mL
Reserved pineapple juice	1/2 cup	125 mL
Soy sauce	2 tbsp.	30 mL
Brown sugar, packed	2 tbsp.	30 mL
Chili sauce	2 tbsp.	30 mL
Ground allspice	1/4 tsp.	1 mL
Large red pepper, seeds and ribs removed, cut into 1 inch (2.5 cm) pieces	1	1
Can of pineapple tidbits (14 oz., 398 mL), drained and juice reserved	1	1
Can of sliced water chestnuts (8 oz., 227 mL), drained	1	1
Water	2 tbsp.	30 mL
Cornstarch	2 tbsp.	30 mL

Put onion and carrots into your slow cooker.

Combine next 4 ingredients in a large resealable freezer bag. Add 1/3 of chicken breast pieces and thighs. Seal bag and toss until chicken is coated. Repeat with remaining chicken. Arrange chicken on top of carrots.

Combine next 6 ingredients in a liquid measure or bowl. Pour over chicken. Do not stir. Cook, covered, on Low for 8 to 9 hours or on High for 4 to 4 1/2 hours.

Stir in red pepper, pineapple and water chestnuts.

Combine water and cornstarch in a small cup, stirring until smooth. Add to chicken mixture and stir well. Cook, covered, on High for about 20 minutes until red pepper is tender-crisp and sauce is slightly thickened. Makes 12 servings.

1 serving: 245 Calories; 4 g Total Fat (1 g Mono, 1 g Poly, 1 g Sat); 105 mg Cholesterol; 19 g Carbohydrate (2 g Fibre, 11 g Sugar); 32 g Protein; 442 mg Sodium

Chicken and Rice

This simple, tasty dish is an essential recipe for any slow cooker repertoire. Cook it on High for best results.

Cooking oil	1 tbsp.	15 mL
Bone-in, skinless chicken thighs	4	4
Chicken drumsticks, skin removed	4	4
Chopped onion	1 cup	250 mL
Garlic cloves, minced (or 1/2 tsp., 2 mL, powder)	2	2
Turmeric	1 tsp.	5 mL
Chili paste (sambal oelek)	1 tsp.	5 mL
Can of diced tomatoes (28 oz., 796 mL), with juice	1	1
Converted white (or brown) rice	1 1/2 cups	375 mL
Prepared chicken broth	1 1/2 cups	375 mL
Chopped red pepper	1 cup	250 mL
Chopped celery	1/2 cup	125 mL
Salt	1/2 tsp.	2 mL
Pepper	1/4 tsp.	1 mL
Frozen peas	2/3 cup	150 mL

Heat cooking oil in a large frying pan on medium. Add chicken thighs and drumsticks. Cook for 8 to 10 minutes, turning occasionally, until browned. Transfer to your slow cooker.

Add onion to same frying pan. Cook for 5 to 10 minutes, stirring often, until softened.

Add garlic, turmeric and chili paste. Heat, stirring, for about 1 minute until fragrant. Add to chicken.

Stir in next 7 ingredients. Cook, covered, on High for 3 1/2 to 4 hours.

Add peas. Stir gently. Cook, covered, on High for 5 to 10 minutes until peas are heated through. Makes 4 servings.

1 serving: 580 Calories; 11 g Total Fat (3 g Mono, 1.5 g Poly, 1 g Sat); 125 mg Cholesterol; 75 g Carbohydrate (4 g Fibre, 10 g Sugar); 43 g Protein; 880 mg Sodium

Chicken Cacciatore

Garlic, onion, wine and herbs give this classic Italian dish incredible flavour. To shake things up a little, try substituting white wine for the red. We prefer to serve this dish over linguini or fettuccini, but you could also pair it with roasted potatoes or basmati rice.

Cooking oil	1 tsp.	5 mL
Bone in chicken pieces, skin removed	1 1/2 lbs.	680 g
Chopped onion	1 cup	250 mL
Sliced mushrooms	1 cup	250 mL
Garlic cloves, minced	2	2
Red wine	1/4 cup	60 mL
Can of diced tomatoes (28 oz., 796 mL), with juice	1	1
Tomato paste	1/4 cup	60 mL
Granulated sugar	1 tsp.	5 mL
Bay leaf	1	1
Dried basil	1 tsp.	5 mL
Dried oregano	1 tsp.	5 mL
Dried rosemary, crushed	1/2 tsp.	2 mL
Salt	1/2 tsp.	2 mL
Pepper	1/4 tsp.	1 mL
Pitted black olives	1 cup	250 mL
Fresh basil, for garnish		
Grated Parmesan cheese, for garnish		

Heat cooking oil in a large frying pan on medium. Add chicken and cook for about 5 minutes, stirring occasionally, until chicken starts to brown.

Add onion and mushrooms and cook, stirring occasionally, until softened. Add garlic and cook, stirring, until fragrant, about 2 minutes.

Add wine. Heat, stirring, for 1 minute. Transfer to your slow cooker.

Combine next 9 ingredients in a medium bowl. Pour over chicken. Cook, covered, on Low for 6 to 7 hours or on High for 3 to 3 1/2 hours.

Remove bay leaf. Stir in olives. Sprinkle individual servings with fresh basil and Parmesan. Makes 6 servings.

1 serving: 230 calories; 7 g Total Fat (3.5 g Mono, 0.5 g Poly, 0 g Sat); 65 mg Cholesterol; 13 g Carbohydrate (2 g Fibre, 7 g Sugar); 28 g Protein; 900 mg Sodium

Lemon Chicken

Quick and easy to prepare in the morning. Present this zesty, aromatic chicken on a large platter, surrounded with colourful rice pilaf.

Whole chicken, rinsed and patted dry (about 3 1/2 lbs., 1.6 kg)	1	1
Garlic cloves, coarsely chopped	4	4
Medium lemon, halved	1	1
Sprig of fresh rosemary	1	1
Dry white (or alcohol-free) wine	1/2 cup	125 mL
Sprigs of fresh rosemary	2	2
Worcestershire sauce	2 tsp.	10 mL
Salt	1/4 tsp.	1 mL
Pepper	1/8 tsp.	0.5 mL
Water	2 tbsp.	30 mL
Chicken gravy thickener	2 tbsp.	30 mL

Carefully loosen, but do not remove, skin around breast, thighs and legs of chicken. Stuff garlic evenly between meat and skin.

Place both lemon halves and first rosemary sprig inside chicken. Tie legs together with butcher's string. Tie wings to body.

Pour wine into your slow cooker and add chicken, breast-side up. Place remaining 2 rosemary sprigs beside chicken, 1 on each side.

Brush Worcestershire sauce evenly over chicken and sprinkle with salt and pepper. Cook, covered, on Low for 8 to 10 hours or on High for 4 to 5 hours. Carefully transfer chicken to a large serving platter and cover with foil. Let stand for 10 minutes. Meanwhile skim and discard any fat from surface of liquid in slow cooker. Strain liquid through a sieve into a small saucepan. Discard solids.

Combine water and gravy thickener in a small cup, stirring until smooth. Slowly add to liquid in saucepan, stirring constantly. Heat and stir on medium for about 5 minutes until boiling and thickened. Remove and discard foil and butcher's string from chicken. Serve with sauce. Makes 4 servings.

1 serving: 706 Calories; 15 g Total Fat (5 g Mono, 3 g Poly, 4 g Sat); 337 mg Cholesterol; 7 g Carbohydrate (1 g Fibre, 1 g Sugar); 124 g Protein; 645 mg Sodium

Moroccan Chicken

Cardamom and cinnamon unite with a variety of spices to produce a spicy, yet subtly sweet taste reminiscent of many Moroccan dishes. Serve over rice or couscous.

Cooking oil	2 tsp.	10 mL
Thinly sliced onion	2 cups	500 mL
Garlic cloves, minced	2	2
(or 1/2 tsp., 2 mL, powder)		
Finely grated ginger root	1/2 tsp.	2 mL
Chili powder	1/2 tsp.	2 mL
Ground coriander	1/2 tsp.	2 mL
Ground cumin	1/2 tsp.	2 mL
Boneless, skinless chicken breast,	1 lb.	454 g
cut into bite size pieces		
Dry white wine (or prepared chicken broth)	1/2 cup	125 mL
Liquid honey	2 tbsp.	30 mL
Cinnamon stick (4 inches, 10 cm)	1	1
Whole green cardamom, bruised	6	6
(see Tip 1, page 91), or 1/4 tsp.		
(1 mL) ground		
Salt, to taste		
Orange juice	1/4 cup	60 mL
Cornstarch	2 tsp.	10 mL
Sesame seeds, toasted	3 tbsp.	45 mL
(see Tip 2, page 91), optional		
Chopped green onion	2 tbsp.	30 mL

Heat cooking oil in a large frying pan on medium. Add next 3 ingredients. Cook for 5 to 10 minutes, stirring often, until onion is softened and starting to brown.

Add next 3 ingredients. Heat, stirring, for 1 to 2 minutes until fragrant. Transfer to your slow cooker.

Stir in next 6 ingredients. Cook, covered, on Low for 7 to 8 hours or on High for 3 1/2 to 4 hours.

Combine orange juice cornstarch in a small bowl, stirring until smooth. Pour over chicken mixture and stir well. Cook, covered, on High for about 15 minutes until boiling and thickened. Remove and discard cinnamon stick and cardamom pods.

Sprinkle with sesame seeds and green onion. Makes 4 servings.

1 serving: 290 Calories; 10 g Total Fat (4.5 g Mono, 2.5 g Poly, 2 g Sat); 94 mg Cholesterol; 22 g Carbohydrate (2 g Fibre, 12 g Sugar); 24 g Protein; 106 mg Sodium

Tip 1: To bruise cardamom, pound the pods with a mallet or press with the flat side of a wide knife to "bruise," or crack them open slightly.

Tip 2: When toasting nuts, seeds or coconut, cooking times will vary for each type of nut, so never toast them together. For small amounts, place the ingredient in an ungreased shallow frying pan. Heat on medium for 3 to 5 minutes, stirring often, until golden. For larger amounts, spread the ingredient evenly in an ungreased shallow pan. Bake in a 350°F (175°C) oven for 5 to 10 minutes, stirring or shaking often, until golden.

Cajun Chicken

With a pot of this hearty sausage and chicken stew, Mardi Gras is just a slow cooker away. Serve over rice.

Cooking oil	2 tbsp.	30 mL
Chopped onion	1 1/2 cups	375 mL
Chopped red pepper	1 cup	250 mL
Chopped celery	1/3 cup	75 mL
Garlic cloves, minced (or 1 tsp., 5 mL, powder)	4	4
All-purpose flour	2 tbsp.	30 mL
Sliced green onion	1/3 cup	75 mL
Lean kielbasa (or smoked ham) sausage ring (10 oz., 285 g), cut into 6 pieces and halved lengthwise	1	1
Boneless, skinless chicken thighs (about 3 oz., 85 g, each)	10	10
Bay leaf	1	1
Can of condensed chicken broth (10 oz., 284 mL)	1	1
Chili sauce	1/2 cup	125 mL
Chili powder	1 1/2 tsp.	7 mL
Dried basil	1/2 tsp.	2 mL
Dried oregano	1/2 tsp.	2 mL
Ground thyme	1/4 tsp.	1 mL
Pepper	1/4 tsp.	1 mL

Heat cooking oil in a large frying pan on medium-high. Add next 4 ingredients and cook for 3 to 4 minutes, stirring often, until onion is softened.

Sprinkle with flour. Heat, stirring, for 1 minute. Transfer to your slow cooker.

Layer next 3 ingredients, in order given, over vegetable mixture. Add bay leaf.

Combine remaining 7 ingredients in same frying pan. Heat, stirring, on medium for 5 minutes, scraping any brown bits from bottom of pan. Pour over chicken. Cook, covered, on Low for 7 to 8 hours or on High for 3 1/2 to 4 hours. Makes 8 servings.

1 serving: 255 Calories; 10 g Total Fat (3.5 g Mono, 2 g Poly, 2 g Sat); 104 mg Cholesterol; 13 g Carbohydrate (1 g Fibre, 6 g Sugar); 28 g Protein; 854 mg Sodium

Creole and Cajun food are two types of cuisine popular in Louisiana. Although they share some of the same ingredients, their origins are quite different. Creole and Cajun are not just types of cuisine, they also represent cultural heritage. A person who is Creole has a multi-racial heritage with African and Caribbean roots. A person who claims Cajun ancestry has ties to the French Acadians who originally settled in modern-day Nova Scotia and moved south. Although both groups relocated to Southern Louisiana, their origins are very different and their cooking is influenced by their original heritage and the local foodstuffs available in Louisiana.

Peanut Butter Chicken Stew

Peanut butter gives this stew a richness and real depth of flavour. Serve it with fresh buttermilk biscuits or crusty bread.

Cooking oil	2 tsp.	10 mL
Chopped celery	1 cup	250 mL
Chopped fresh white mushrooms	1 cup	250 mL
Chopped onion, sliced	2	2
Garlic cloves, minced	2	2
(or 1/2 tsp., 2 mL, powder)		
Paprika	1/2 tsp.	2 mL
Pepper	1/2 tsp.	2 mL
Chopped carrot	2 cups	500 mL
Bone-in chicken thighs (about 5 oz.,	3 1/2 lbs.	1.6 kg
140 g, each), skin removed (see Note)		
Can of tomato sauce (7 1/2 oz., 213 mL)	1	1
Brown sugar, packed	1 tbsp.	15 mL
Curry powder	1 tsp.	5 mL
Peanut butter	1/2 cup	125 mL
Plain yogurt (full fat)	1/2 cup	125 mL
Fresh (or frozen) whole green beans,	2 cups	500 mL
quartered		
Coarsely chopped unsalted	2 tbsp.	30 mL
peanuts (optional)		

Heat cooking oil in a large frying pan on medium. Add next 6 ingredients and cook for 8 to 10 minutes, stirring often, until mushrooms and onion are softened and starting to brown. Transfer to your slow cooker.

Layer carrots and chicken, in order given, over onion mixture.

Combine next 3 ingredients in a small bowl and pour over chicken. Cook, covered, on Low for 6 to 7 hours or on High for 3 to 3 1/2 hours.

Combine peanut butter and yogurt in a small bowl. Add to slow cooker and stir well. Stir in green beans. Cook, covered, on High for about 10 minutes until beans are tender crisp.

Sprinkle with peanuts, if using. Makes about 9 cups.

1 cup (250 mL): 200 Calories; 11 g Total Fat (1 g Mono, 0.5 g Poly, 2.5 g Sat); 45 mg Cholesterol; 13 g Carbohydrate (3 g Fibre; 7 g Sugar); 15 g Protein; 310 mg Sodium

Note: Use whichever cuts of chicken you prefer as long as the weight used is equal to that listed.

Pesto Chicken Pasta

Light, mildly spiced sauce coats pasta, red pepper and chicken.

Chopped red onion	1 cup	250 mL
Dry white (or alcohol-free) wine	1 cup	250 mL
Red medium peppers, seeds and ribs removed, chopped	2	2
Garlic cloves, minced (or 1/2 tsp., 2 mL, powder)	2	2
Chili powder	1 tsp.	5 mL
Salt	1/2 tsp.	2 mL
Pepper	1/2 tsp.	2 mL
Boneless, skinless chicken breasts, cut into strips	4	4
Lemon juice	1 tbsp.	15 mL
Cornstarch	1 tbsp.	15 mL
Sun-dried tomato pesto	3 tbsp.	45 mL
Penne pasta (about 10 oz., 285 g)	3 cups	750 mL
Sliced green olives, optional		
Chopped sun-dried tomatoes, packed in oil, optional		
Grated Parmesan cheese	1/3 cup	75 mL

Combine first 7 ingredients in your slow cooker. Add chicken and stir well. Cook, covered, on Low for 7 to 8 hours or on High for 3 1/2 to 4 hours.

Combine lemon juice and cornstarch in a small cup, stirring until smooth. Stir in pesto. Add to chicken mixture, stirring well. Cook, covered, on High for about 15 minutes until sauce is thickened.

Cook pasta according to package directions until tender but firm. Drain and return pasta to pot. Add chicken mixture. Toss gently until coated. Transfer to a large serving bowl.

Sprinkle with olives, sun-dried tomatoes and Parmesan cheese. Makes 6 servings.

1 serving: 470 Calories; 11 g Total Fat (2.5 g Mono, 1.5 g Poly, 3 g Sat); 100 mg Cholesterol; 52 g Carbohydrate (3 g Fibre, 6 g Sugar); 33 g Protein; 430 mg Sodium

Beer and Bacon Chicken

Delightfully tender chicken in a smoky bacon and beer sauce. Delicious served with buttered carrots and mashed potatoes.

All-purpose flour	3 tbsp.	45 mL
Chicken drumsticks, skin removed	12	12
Bacon slices, cooked crisp and crumbled	4	4
Can of beer (12 1/2 oz., 355 mL)	1	1
Prepared chicken broth	1/2 cup	125 mL
Worcestershire sauce	1 tbsp.	15 mL
Chopped fresh oregano leaves (or 3/4 tsp., 4 mL, dried)	1 tbsp.	15 mL
Chopped fresh thyme leaves (or 1/2 tsp., 2 mL, dried)	2 tsp.	10 mL
Salt	1/4 tsp.	1 mL
Pepper	1/4 tsp.	1 mL
Water	1 tbsp.	15 mL
Cornstarch	2 tsp.	10 mL

Measure flour into a large resealable freezer bag. Add 1/2 of chicken. Seal bag and toss until chicken is coated. Repeat with remaining chicken. Put chicken into your slow cooker.

Combine next 8 ingredients in a large liquid measure or bowl. Pour over chicken and stir. Cook, covered, on Low for 8 to 9 hours or on High for 4 to 4 1/2 hours. Carefully transfer chicken with a slotted spoon to a large serving bowl. Cover to keep warm.

Combine water and cornstarch in a small cup, stirring until smooth. Add to liquid in slow cooker. Stir well. Cook, covered, on High for about 15 minutes until thickened. Pour over chicken. Makes 6 servings.

1 serving: 234 Calories; 8.9 g Total Fat (3.1 g Mono, 1.9 g Poly, 2.5 g Sat); 98 mg Cholesterol; 7 g Carbohydrate; trace Fibre; 26 g Protein; 268 mg Sodium

Chicken a la King

Green pepper and pimiento give this attractive dish a splash of colour. Serve over rice or noodles, or for an elegant presentation, serve in pastry cups.

Finely chopped celery	1/4 cup	60 mL
Chopped onion	1/2 cup	125 mL
Medium green pepper, diced	1	1
Small fresh mushrooms, sliced	3 cups	750 mL
Jar of chopped pimiento (2 oz., 57 mL) drained	1	1
Boneless, skinless chicken breast halves, chopped	4	4
All-purpose flour	6 tbsp.	90 mL
Salt	1 tsp.	5 mL
Pepper	1/4 tsp.	1 mL
Milk	1 1/2 cups	375 mL
Sherry (or alcohol-free sherry)	1/4 cup	60 mL

Combine first 5 ingredients in your slow cooker. Scatter chicken over top.

Combine flour, salt and pepper in a saucepan. Whisk in milk gradually until no lumps remain. Heat, stirring, until boiling and thickened. Mixture will be quite thick.

Stir in sherry. Pour over chicken. Cook, covered, on Low for 6 to 8 hours or on High for 3 to 4 hours. If chicken pieces have stuck together, break apart before serving. Makes 6 cups (1.5 L).

1 cup (250 mL): 170 Calories; 2 g Total Fat (0 g Mono, 0 g Poly, 0.5 g Sat); 50 mg Cholesterol; 14 g Carbohydrate (1 g Fibre, 6 g Sugar); 23 g Protein; 490 mg Sodium

Chicken-Stuffed Peppers

Vibrant red peppers brimming with ground turkey and brown rice create a hearty, yet light meal with lean ingredients.

Large red peppers	6	6
Canola oil	2 tsp.	10 mL
Lean ground chicken	1 lb.	454 g
Chopped celery	1 cup	250 mL
Chopped onion	1 cup	250 mL
Garlic cloves, minced (or 1/2 tsp., 2 mL, powder)	2	2
Cooked long-grain brown rice (about 2/3 cup, 150 mL, uncooked)	2 cups	500 mL
Can of diced tomatoes (with juice)	14 oz.	398 mL
Chopped fresh parsley (or 1 1/2 tsp., 7 mL, flakes)	1/4 cup	60 mL
Sliced green onion	1/4 cup	60 mL
Grated lemon zest	1 tsp.	5 mL
Grated orange zest	1/2 tsp.	2 mL
Ground allspice	1/2 tsp.	2 mL
Salt	1/4 tsp.	1 mL
Pepper	1/4 tsp.	1 mL
Water	1 1/2 cups	375 mL

Cut 1/2 inch (12 mm) from top of each red pepper. Remove seeds and ribs. Trim bottom of each pepper so it will sit flat, being careful not to cut into cavity. Set aside. Dice tops of peppers surrounding stem. Discard stems.

Heat canola oil in large frying pan on medium-high. Add turkey. Scramble-fry for about 7 minutes until turkey is no longer pink.

Add next 3 ingredients. Cook for about 5 minutes, stirring often, until celery is softened. Remove from heat.

Add next 9 ingredients and diced red pepper. Stir. Spoon into prepared peppers. Arrange upright in 7 quart (7 L) slow cooker.

Pour water around stuffed peppers. Cook, covered, on Low for 4 to 5 hours or on High for 2 to 2 1/2 hours. Makes 6 stuffed peppers.

1 stuffed pepper: 460 Calories; 14 g Total Fat (1 g Mono, 0.5 g Poly, 0 g Sat); 55 mg Cholesterol; 67 g Carbohydrate; (9 g Fibre; 11 g Sugar); 20 g Protein; 360 mg Sodium

Chicken Chickpea Stew

This fragrant stew is loaded with chicken, chickpeas, pepperoni and tender vegetables. Rich and filling, it is the perfect comfort food for a cool autumn evening.

Boneless, skinless chicken breast halves (about 5 oz., 140 g, each), each cut into 2 pieces	12	12
Can of chickpeas (19 oz., 540 mL), rinsed and drained	1	1
Sliced carrot	1 2/3 cups	400 mL
Chopped onion	1 cup	250 mL
Chopped green pepper	1 cup	250 mL
Deli pepperoni sticks, cut into 1/2 inch (12 mm) pieces	4 oz.	113 g
Can of tomato paste (5 1/2 oz., 156 mL)	1	1
Water	2/3 cup	150 mL
Medium sherry	1/4 cup	60 mL
Salt	1/2 tsp.	2 mL
Chopped fresh basil (or 3/4 tsp., 4 mL, dried), see Note	1 tbsp.	15 mL
Chopped fresh thyme leaves (or 1/4 tsp., 1 mL, dried), see Note	1 tsp.	5 mL
Chopped fresh parsley (or 1/4 tsp., 1 mL, flakes), see Note	1 tsp.	5 mL

Layer first 6 ingredients, in order given, in your slow cooker.

Combine next 4 ingredients in a small bowl. Pour over pepperoni. Do not stir. Cook, covered, on Low for 8 to 9 hours or on High for 4 to 4 1/2 hours.

Add remaining 3 ingredients and stir well. Cook, covered, on High for about 5 minutes until herbs are fragrant. Makes 6 servings.

1 serving: 500 Calories; 10 g Total Fat (0.5 g Mono, 0.5 g Poly, 1 g Sat); 150 mg Cholesterol; 32 g Carbohydrate (9 g Fibre, 7 g Sugar); 67 g Protein; 880 mg Sodium

Note: If using dried herbs instead of fresh, add them to the tomato paste mixture.

Mild Turkey Chili

Ground turkey replaces the beef in this colourful dish, giving it a lighter flavour than traditional chili. Serve with tortilla chips or crusty bread.

Cooking oil	2 tsp.	10 mL
Chopped onion	1 cup	250 mL
Chopped red pepper	1 cup	250 mL
Chili powder	1 tsp.	5 mL
Paprika	1 tsp.	5 mL
Ground cumin	1 tsp.	5 mL
Salt	1/4 tsp.	1 mL
Lean ground turkey	1 1/2 lbs.	680 g
Cans of red kidney beans (14 oz., 398 mL, each), rinsed and drained	2	2
Can of diced tomatoes (14 oz., 398 mL) with juice	1	1
Tomato paste (see Tip, page 38)	2 tbsp.	30 mL
Diced jalapeño pepper, seeds and ribs removed (see Tip, page 124)	1 tbsp.	15 mL
Chopped fresh cilantro or parsley (or 1 1/2 tsp., 7 mL, dried)	2 tbsp.	30 mL

Heat cooking oil in a large frying pan on medium. Add onion and red pepper. Cook for 5 to 10 minutes, stirring often, until onion is softened.

Add next 4 ingredients. Heat, stirring, for about 1 minute until fragrant.

Add ground turkey and scramble-fry on medium-high for 5 to 10 minutes until turkey is no longer pink. Drain and transfer to your slow cooker.

Stir in next 4 ingredients. Cook, covered, on Low for 10 to 11 hours or on High for 5 to 5 1/2 hours.

Add cilantro. Stir well. Makes 6 servings.

1 serving: 280 Calories; 9 g Total Fat (1 g Mono, 0.5 g Poly, 1 g Sat); 60 mg Cholesterol; 25 g Carbohydrate (10 g Fibre, 5 g Sugar); 29 g Protein; 590 mg Sodium

Turkey Roast Supreme

Take turkey back from the holidays and start making it weekday fare. This turkey roast cooks up juicy and tender in the slow cooker. The leftovers make amazing sandwiches.

Baby carrots	2 cups	500 mL
Sliced celery	1 2/3 cups	400 mL
Olive (or cooking) oil	1 tbsp.	15 mL
Sliced onion	1 1/2 cups	375 mL
Garlic cloves, minced (or 1/2 tsp., 2 mL, powder)	2	2
Olive (or cooking) oil	1 tsp.	5 mL
Paprika	1 tsp.	5 mL
Pepper	1 tsp.	5 mL
Turkey breast roast (about 2 1/2 lbs., 1.1 kg)	1	1
Prepared chicken broth	1 cup	250 mL
Italian no-salt seasoning	2 tsp.	10 mL
Evaporated milk	3/4 cup	175 mL
All-purpose flour	2 tbsp.	30 mL

Layer carrots and celery, in order given, in your slow cooker.

Heat first amount of olive oil in a large frying pan on medium. Add onion and cook for about 10 minutes, stirring often, until onion is softened and starting to brown. Add to slow cooker.

Combine next 4 ingredients in a small dish. Rub spice mixture on roast and place roast over onion in slow cooker.

Pour broth around roast. Sprinkle with seasoning. Cook, covered, on Low for 7 to 8 hours or on High for 3 1/2 to 4 hours. Transfer roast to a cutting board. Cover with foil and let stand for 10 minutes.

Combine evaporated milk and flour in a small bowl, stirring until smooth. Add to slow cooker. Cook, covered, on High for about 15 minutes until boiling and slightly thickened. Cut roast into thin slices. Arrange on a serving platter and spoon vegetables and sauce over top. Makes 8 servings.

1 serving: 300 Calories; 13 g Total Fat (5 g Mono, 2.5 g Poly, 3.5 g Sat); 90 mg Cholesterol; 11 g Carbohydrate (2 g Fibre, 5 g Sugar); 34 g Protein; 230 mg Sodium

Jambalaya

Shrimp, chicken, sausage and juicy vegetables—there's something for everyone in this spicy rice dish!

Boneless, skinless chicken thighs (about 3 oz., 85 g, each), halved	8	8
Cooking oil	1 tsp.	5 mL
Chorizo sausage, cut into 1/2 inch (12 mm) slices	1 lb.	454 g
Can of diced tomatoes (14 oz., 398 mL), with juice	1	1
Chopped green pepper	1 1/2 cups	375 mL
Chopped onion	1 cup	250 mL
Chopped celery	1 cup	250 mL
Can of tomato sauce (7 1/2 oz., 213 mL)	1	1
Garlic cloves, minced (or 1/2 tsp., 2 mL, powder)	2	2
Dried basil	1/2 tsp.	2 mL
Paprika	1/2 tsp.	2 mL
Dried crushed chilies	1/2 tsp.	2 mL
Dried thyme	1/4 tsp.	1 mL
Cooked long grain white rice (about 3/4 cup, 175 mL, uncooked)	2 cups	500 mL
Fresh uncooked medium shrimp, peeled and deveined	1 lb.	454 g

Place chicken in your slow cooker.

Heat cooking oil in a large frying pan on medium. Add sausage and cook for about 5 minutes, stirring occasionally, until starting to brown. Transfer to paper towels to drain.

Combine next 10 ingredients in a large bowl. Pour over chicken. Stir in sausage. Cook, covered, on Low for 8 to 9 hours or on High for 4 to 4 1/2 hours.

Add rice and shrimp. Stir gently. Cook, covered, on High for 15 to 20 minutes until shrimp are pink and curled. Makes 8 servings.

1 serving: 480 Calories; 24 g Total Fat (.5 g Mono, .5 g Poly, 6 g Sat); 200 mg Cholesterol; 19 g Carbohydrate (2 g Fibre, 4 g Sugar); 43 g Protein; 760 mg Sodium

Shrimp Creole

Tender shrimp pairs perfectly with green pepper, tomato and mushrooms in this colourful dish. Serve over a long grain rice, such as basmati.

Finely chopped onion	1 cup	250 mL
Chopped celery	1/2 cup	125 mL
Medium green pepper, chopped	1	1
Canned tomatoes (14 oz., 398 mL), with juice, broken up	1	1
Ketchup	2 tbsp.	30 mL
Can of sliced mushrooms (10 oz., 284 mL), drained	1	1
Salt	1 tsp.	5 mL
Pepper	1/4 tsp.	1 mL
Garlic powder	1/4 tsp.	1 mL
Cayenne pepper	1/4 tsp.	1 mL
Lemon juice	1 tsp.	5 mL
Parsley flakes	1 tsp.	5 mL
Cooked fresh (or cooked frozen, thawed) shelled shrimp (or 2 cans, 4 oz., 114 g, each, drained)	1 lb.	454 g

Put onion, celery and green pepper into your slow cooker.

Combine next 9 ingredients in a bowl. Pour over top of onion mixture. Cook, covered, on Low for 6 to 8 hours or on High for 3 to 4 hours.

Stir in shrimp. Cook on High for 20 to 30 minutes until shrimp is heated through. Stir before serving. Makes 4 1/4 cups (1 L).

1 cup (250 mL): 180 Calories; 2 g Total Fat (0 g Mono, 1 g Poly, 0 g Sat); 160 mg Cholesterol; 15 g Carbohydrate (3 g Fibre, 8 g Sugar); 25 g Protein; 1020 mg Sodium

Shrimp Marinara

Delicious shrimp in an Italian spiced sauce. Serve over rice or pasta, and garnish with fresh basil.

Canned tomatoes (14 oz., 398 mL), with juice, broken up	1	1
Finely chopped onion	1 cup	250 mL
Garlic cloves, minced (or 1/2 tsp., 2 mL, powder)	2	2
Dried oregano	3/4 tsp.	4 mL
Salt	1 tsp.	5 mL
Pepper	1/4 tsp.	1 mL
Parsley flakes	1/2 tsp.	2 mL
Granulated sugar	1/2 tsp.	2 mL
Cooked fresh (or cooked frozen, thawed) shelled shrimp	1 lb.	454 g
Grated Parmesan cheese, optional		

Combine first 8 ingredients in your slow cooker. Cook, covered, on Low for 6 to 7 hours or on High for 3 to 3 1/2 hours until onion is cooked.

Stir in shrimp. Cook on High for about 15 minutes until heated through.

Spoon over rice or pasta. Sprinkle with cheese, if using. Makes 3 1/3 cups (825 mL).

3/4 cup (175 mL): 130 Calories; 1 g Total Fat (0 g Mono, 0 g Poly, 0 g Sat); 185 mg Cholesterol; 8 g Carbohydrate (1 g Fibre, 4 g Sugar); 21 g Protein; 890 mg Sodium

Tip: Don't be tempted to lift the lid on your slow cooker and give the contents a stir unless a recipe specifically asks you to do so. The lid actually becomes vacuum sealed by the heat and steam. If you lift the lid, the steam will escape, which can add to your cooking time.

Seafood Casserole

This casserole has a mild seafood flavor with a golden cheese topping. The splash of sherry adds wonderful flavour to the shrimp and crabmeat.

Can of condensed cream of mushroom soup (10 oz., 284 mL)	1	1
Water	1 cup	250 mL
Sherry (or alcohol-free sherry)	2 tbsp.	30 mL
Jars of chopped pimiento (2 oz., 57 mL each), drained	2	2
Onion flakes	1 tbsp.	15 mL
Dill weed	1/2 tsp.	2 mL
Paprika	1/2 tsp.	2 mL
Parsley flakes	1 tsp.	5 mL
Cayenne pepper	1/8 tsp.	0.5 mL
Frozen shrimp, thawed, drained and chopped	4 oz.	113 g
Can of crabmeat (4.2 oz., 120 g) drained, cartilage removed	1	1
Uncooked converted white rice	1 1/2 cups	375 mL
Grated medium Cheddar cheese	1 cup	250 mL

Mix first 9 ingredients in a bowl.

Place shrimp, crabmeat and rice in your slow cooker. Pour soup mixture over top and stir lightly. Sprinkle with cheese. Cook, covered, on Low for 3 to 4 hours or on High for 1 1/2 to 2 hours. Makes 5 cups (1.25 L).

1 cup (250 mL): 410 Calories; 12 g Total Fat (3 g Mono, 1.5 g Poly, 6 g Sat); 80 mg Cholesterol; 51 g Carbohydrate (1 g Fibre, 1 g Sugar); 21 g Protein; 650 mg Sodium

Lentil Rice Rolls

Flavours of the world unite in these interesting cabbage rolls. Definitely worth a try when you're looking for something a bit different.

Medium head of green cabbage (about 3 lbs., 1.4 kg)	1	1
Can of lentils (19 oz., 540 mL), rinsed and drained	1	1
Can of tomato sauce (7 1/2 oz., 213 mL)	1	1
Long grain brown (or white) rice	1/2 cup	125 mL
Finely chopped carrot	1/2 cup	125 mL
Finely chopped celery	1/2 cup	125 mL
Finely chopped onion	1/2 cup	125 mL
Garlic clove, minced (or 1/4 tsp., 1 mL, powder)	1	1
Dried whole oregano	1/2 tsp.	2 mL
Can of tomato sauce (25 oz., 680 mL)	1	1
Dark raisins	1/4 cup	60 mL
Lemon juice	3 tbsp.	45 mL
Brown sugar, packed	2 tbsp.	30 mL
Grated lemon zest	2 tsp.	10 mL
Ground cinnamon	1/2 tsp.	2 mL

Remove 10 larger outer leaves from cabbage head and place them in a large bowl. Add boiling water until 2 inches (5 cm) above leaves. Let stand for about 5 minutes until softened. Cut a "V" shape with a knife along tough ribs of cabbage leaves to remove. Discard ribs and set leaves aside. Shred remaining cabbage and place in your slow cooker.

Combine next 8 ingredients in a large bowl. Spoon about 1/3 cup (75 mL) lentil mixture onto centre of each cabbage leaf. Fold sides of leaves over filling. Roll up each tightly from bottom to enclose filling. Makes 10 cabbage rolls.

Combine remaining 6 ingredients in a medium bowl. Add 1 1/2 cups (375 mL) tomato sauce mixture to shredded cabbage in slow cooker. Stir well and spread evenly in slow cooker. Arrange rolls, seam-side down, on top of cabbage mixture. Pour remaining tomato sauce mixture on top of rolls. Cook, covered, on Low for 8 to 10 hours or on High for 4 to 5 hours. Carefully transfer rolls to a large plate. Transfer cabbage mixture to a large serving platter and arrange rolls on top. Makes 10 servings.

1 serving: 170 Calories; 1 g Total Fat (0 g Mono, 0 g Poly, 0 g Sat); 0 mg Cholesterol; 36 g Carbohydrate (6 g Fibre, 15 g Sugar); 7 g Protein; 630 mg Sodium

Tomato Chickpea Pasta

This spicy chickpea and tomato sauce tossed with penne pasta is a great meatless option the whole family will love.

Can of diced tomatoes (28 oz., 796 mL) with juice	1	1
Can of chickpeas (19 oz., 540 mL), rinsed and drained	1	1
Dry white (or alcohol-free) wine	1/2 cup	125 mL
Olive (or cooking) oil	2 tbsp.	30 mL
Balsamic vinegar	1 tbsp.	15 mL
Garlic cloves, minced (or 1/2 tsp., 2 mL, powder)	2	2
Dried crushed chilies	1/2 tsp.	2 mL
Granulated sugar	1/2 tsp.	2 mL
Salt	1/4 tsp.	1 mL
Pepper	1/4 tsp.	1 mL
Chopped fresh parsley (or 2 tsp., 10 mL, flakes)	3 tbsp.	45 mL
Penne pasta (about 10 oz., 285 g)	3 cups	750 mL
Grated Parmesan cheese	1/3 cup	75 mL

Combine first 10 ingredients in your slow cooker. Cook, covered, on Low for 8 to 9 hours or on High for 4 to 4 1/2 hours.

Stir in parsley.

Cook pasta according to package directions until tender but firm. Drain and return pasta to pot. Add tomato mixture and toss until coated. Transfer to a large serving bowl.

Sprinkle with Parmesan cheese. Makes 6 servings.

1 serving: 390 Calories; 8 g Total Fat (4 g Mono, 0.5 g Poly, 1.5 g Sat); 5 mg Cholesterol; 62 g Carbohydrate (5 g Fibre, 9 g Sugar); 14 g Protein; 780 mg Sodium

Squash and Dumplings

A subtly spiced, meatless stew topped with cheesy cornmeal dumplings. Enticing Italian flavour and a variety of textures make this dish particularly pleasing!

Butternut squash, cut into 1/2 inch (12 mm) pieces (about 3 cups, 750 mL)	3/4 lb.	340 g
Cans of Italian-style stewed tomatoes (14 oz., 398 mL, each)	2	2
Can of mixed beans (19 oz., 540 mL), rinsed and drained	1	1
Small fresh white mushrooms, halved	2 cups	500 mL
Water	1 cup	250 mL
Garlic cloves, minced (or 1/2 tsp., 2 mL, powder)	2	2
Italian seasoning	2 tsp.	10 mL
Pepper	1/4 tsp.	1 mL
All-purpose flour	1/2 cup	125 mL
Yellow cornmeal	1/3 cup	75 mL
Grated Parmesan cheese	2 tbsp.	30 mL
Baking powder	1 tsp.	5 mL
Paprika	1/8 tsp.	0.5 mL
Large egg	1	1
Milk	2 tbsp.	30 mL
Cooking oil	2 tbsp.	30 mL
Basil pesto	1 tsp.	5 mL

Combine first 8 ingredients in your slow cooker. Cook, covered, on Low for 8 to 9 hours or on High for 4 to 4 1/2 hours.

For the dumplings, combine next 5 ingredients in a medium bowl. Make a well in centre.

Beat remaining 4 ingredients with a fork in a small cup. Add to well and stir until just moistened. Spoon mounds of batter, using 2 tbsp. (30 mL) for each, in a single layer on top of squash mixture. Cook, covered, on High for 40 to 50 minutes a until wooden pick inserted in centre of a dumpling comes out clean. Makes 6 servings.

1 serving: 300 Calories; 7 g Total Fat (3.5 g Mono, 1.5 g Poly, 1.5 g Sat); 40 mg Cholesterol; 50 g Carbohydrate (8 g Fibre, 9 g Sugar); 12 g Protein; 530 mg Sodium

Chili Black Beans

A colourful, spicy blend of veggies and beans. Add a dollop of sour cream or salsa and sprinkle with green onion or cilantro, if desired.

Cans of black beans (19 oz., 540 mL, each), rinsed and drained	2	2
Chopped butternut squash	2 cups	500 mL
Can of diced tomatoes (14 oz., 398 mL), with juice	1	1
Chopped onion	1 1/2 cups	375 mL
Prepared vegetable broth	1/2 cup	125 mL
Jalapeño pepper (with seeds), finely diced (see Tip, below)	1	1
Chili powder	1 tbsp.	15 mL
Bay leaves	2	2
Garlic cloves, minced (or 1/2 tsp., 2 mL, powder)	2	2
Salt	1/4 tsp.	1 mL
Chopped green pepper	1 cup	250 mL

Combine first 10 ingredients in your slow cooker. Cook, covered, on Low for 8 to 10 hours or on High for 4 to 5 hours.

Add green pepper and stir gently. Cook, covered, on High for about 20 minutes until green pepper is tender-crisp. Remove and discard bay leaves. Makes 6 servings.

1 serving: 245 Calories; 2 g Total Fat (0 g Mono, 0 g Poly, 0 g Sat); 0 mg Cholesterol; 47 g Carbohydrate (11 g Fibre, 7 g Sugar); 15 g Protein; 720 mg Sodium

Tip: To reduce the heat in chili peppers and jalapeño peppers, remove the seeds and ribs. Wear rubber gloves and do not touch your eyes when handling hot peppers. Wash your hands well afterwards.

Ratatouille

It may have started out as a way for peasants in the Nice area of France to use up vegetables that were a little past their prime, but ratatouille has become a favourite vegetarian dish that graces the menu of many high-end restaurants around the world. This stew tastes best when made with fresh vegetables, so if you have access to fresh garden tomatoes, leave out the canned tomatoes and use 4 medium diced tomatoes in their place.

Can of tomatoes (19 oz., 540 mL), with juice, broken up		
Small eggplant, with peel, cut into 1/2 inch (12 mm) cubes	1	1
Finely chopped onion	1 cup	250 mL
Chopped celery	1 cup	250 mL
Medium green or red pepper, chopped	1	1
Chili sauce, optional	1/4 cup	60 mL
Granulated sugar	2 tsp.	10 mL
Sliced zucchini, with peel (1/4 inch, 6 mm, thick)	3 cups	750 mL
Parsley flakes	1 tsp.	5 mL
Salt	1/2 tsp.	2 mL
Pepper	1/8 tsp.	0.5 mL
Garlic powder	1/4 tsp.	1 mL
Dried rosemary	1/2 tsp.	2 mL
Dried whole oregano	1/4 tsp.	1 mL
Dried sweet basil	1/2 tsp.	2 mL

Combine all 15 ingredients in your slow cooker. Cook, covered, on Low for 8 to 9 hours or on High for 4 to 4 1/2 hours. Makes 6 1/2 cups (1.6 L).

1 cup (250 mL): 80 Calories; 0 g Total Fat (0 g Mono, 0 g Poly, 0 g Sat); 0 mg Cholesterol; 18 g Carbohydrate (5 g Fibre, 10 g Sugar); 3 g Protein; 530 mg Sodium

Rice and Bean Tacos

Wild rice gives the hearty, meatless taco filling a slight nutty flavour. Top with your favourite fixings, such as lettuce, sliced tomato, onion, sour cream, guacamole and grated cheese.

Cans of mixed beans (19 oz., 540 mL, each), rinsed and drained	2	2
Can of diced tomatoes (28 oz., 796 mL), with juice	1	1
Prepared vegetable broth	1 cup	250 mL
Wild rice	1/2 cup	125 mL
Can of diced green chillies (4 oz., 113 g)	1	1
Chili powder	2 tsp.	10 mL
Granulated sugar	1 tsp.	5 mL
Ground cumin	1 tsp.	5 mL
Dried whole oregano	1 tsp.	5 mL
Pepper	1/2 tsp.	2 mL
Taco shells	24	24

Combine first 10 ingredients in your slow cooker. Cook, covered, on Low for 8 to 10 hours or on High for 4 to 5 hours.

Heat taco shells according to package directions. Spoon 1/4 cup (60 mL) filling into each shell. Top with your choice of fixings. Makes 24 tacos.

1 taco: 130 Calories; 5 g Total Fat (0.5 g Mono, 0 g Poly, 2 g Sat); 10 mg Cholesterol; 17 g Carbohydrate (2 g Fibre, 1 g Sugar); 5 g Protein; 200 mg Sodium

Cauliflower Dhal

Treat the ones you love to this spicy, traditional East Indian dish. Perfect with pappadum, an East Indian flatbread.

Cauliflower florets	4 cups	1 L
Chopped peeled potato	2 cups	500 mL
Yellow split peas, rinsed and drained	1 cup	250 mL
Medium carrots, chopped	2	2
Medium chopped onion	1 cup	250 mL
Garlic clove, minced (or 1/4 tsp., 1 mL, powder)	1	1
Prepared vegetable broth	3 cups	750 mL
Balsamic vinegar	2 tbsp.	30 mL
Red curry paste	1 tsp.	5 mL
Turmeric	1/4 tsp.	1 mL
Ground ginger	1/4 tsp.	1 mL
Ground nutmeg	1/4 tsp.	1 mL
Salt	1/2 tsp.	2 mL
Pepper	1/2 tsp.	2 mL
Fresh spinach, stems removed, lightly packed	1 cup	250 mL

Combine first 6 ingredients in your slow cooker.

Combine remaining 6 ingredients in a medium bowl. Pour over cauliflower mixture and stir well. Cook, covered, on Low for 8 to 9 hours or on High for 4 to 4 1/2 hours. Makes about 7 1/2 cups (1.9 L).

1 cup (250 mL): 150 Calories; 0.5 g Total Fat (0 g Mono, 0 g Poly, 0 g Sat); 0 mg Cholesterol; 27 g Carbohydrate (5 g Fibre, 6 g Sugar); 8 g Protein; 450 mg Sodium

Vegetable Curry

This colourful combination of chickpeas and vegetables is seasoned with a mellow blend of ginger, curry and coconut milk.

Can of coconut milk (14 oz., 398 mL)	1	1
Curry powder	2 tsp.	10 mL
All-purpose flour	1 1/2 tbsp.	25 mL
Cauliflower florets	3 cups	750 mL
Chopped peeled potato	3 cups	750 mL
Can of chickpeas (19 oz., 540 mL), rinsed and drained	1	1
Chopped carrot	2 cups	500 mL
Chopped onion	1 2/3 cups	400 mL
Finely grated, peeled ginger root	1 tbsp.	15 mL
Garlic cloves, minced (or 1/2 tsp., 2 mL, powder)	2	2
Salt	1 tsp.	5 mL
Frozen peas	1/2 cup	125 mL

Beat first 3 ingredients with a whisk in a small bowl until smooth.

Put next 8 ingredients into your slow cooker. Add coconut milk mixture and stir well. Cook, covered, on Low for 7 to 8 hours or on High for 3 1/2 to 4 hours.

Gently stir in peas. Cook, covered, on High for 5 to 10 minutes until peas are heated through. Makes 8 servings.

1 serving: 190 Calories; 11 g Total Fat (0 g Mono, 0 g Poly, 9 g Sat); 0 mg Cholesterol; 23 g Carbohydrate (4 g Fibre, 6 g Sugar); 4 g Protein; 370 mg Sodium

Sufferin' Succotash

Succotash is an American dish, common in the South, that is traditionally prepared with fresh lima beans and sweet corn. It is most often eaten in late summer, when fresh corn is at its best. This recipe uses frozen corn instead of fresh, but if you have access to fresh corn in season, use it instead.

Frozen lima beans	2 cups	500 mL
Chopped onion	1 1/2 cups	375 mL
Sliced celery	1/2 cup	125 mL
Frozen corn	2 cups	500 mL
Chopped pimiento	2 tbsp.	30 mL
Garlic powder	1/4 tsp.	1 mL
Dried sweet basil	1/4 tsp.	1 mL
Salt	1/2 tsp.	2 mL
Pepper, to taste		
Can of condensed cream of mushroom soup (10 oz., 284 mL)	1	1

Grated medium Cheddar cheese, sprinkle

Combine first 10 ingredients in a large bowl, stirring well. Transfer to your slow cooker. Cook, covered, on Low for 8 to 10 hours or on High for 4 to 5 hours.

Stir well and sprinkle with cheese before serving. Makes 4 cups (1 L).

1/2 cup (125 mL): 120 Calories; 3 g Total Fat (1 g Mono, 0 g Poly, 1 g Sat); 5 mg Cholesterol; 21 g Carbohydrate (3 g Fibre, 4 g Sugar); 5 g Protein; 530 mg Sodium

Boston Baked Beans

Traditionally, Boston baked beans were made with diced salt pork, but you won't miss it in this vegetarian version, which is rich with molasses and brown sugar.

Dried navy beans (or peas)	2 1/4 cups	560 mL
Chopped onion	1 1/2 cups	375 mL
Water	5 cups	1.25 L
Ketchup	1/2 cup	125 mL
Molasses (not blackstrap)	1/3 cup	75 mL
Brown sugar, packed	1/3 cup	75 mL
Dry mustard	1 tsp.	5 mL
Salt	1 tsp.	5 mL
Pepper	1/4 tsp.	1 mL

Combine beans, onion and water in your slow cooker. Cook, covered, on Low for 8 to 10 hours or on High for 4 to 5 hours. Do not drain.

Add remaining 6 ingredients. Stir well. Cook, covered, on High for 2 to 3 hours or on Low for 4 to 6 hours to blend flavours. Makes 6 cups (1.5 L).

1/2 cup (125 mL): 200 Calories; 0.5 g Total Fat (0 g Mono, 0 g Poly, 0 g Sat); 0 mg Cholesterol; 41 g Carbohydrate (7 g Fibre, 17 g Sugar); 9 g Protein; 340 mg Sodium

White Bread

This bread has the same homemade aroma and flavour as regular bread, but the texture is a touch more porous.

Granulated sugar	2 tsp.	10 mL
Warm water	1 1/4 cups	300 mL
Envelope active dry yeast (1/4 oz., 8 g) (1 scant tbsp., 15 mL)	1	1
All-purpose flour	2 cups	500 mL
Granulated sugar	2 tbsp.	30 mL
Cooking oil	2 tbsp.	30 mL
Salt	1 tsp.	5 mL
All-purpose flour	1 cup	250 mL

Stir first amount of sugar and warm water together in a large bowl. Sprinkle with yeast and let stand for 10 minutes. Stir to dissolve yeast.

Add next 4 ingredients and beat on low to moisten. Beat on high for 2 minutes.

Knead in second amount of flour until a stiff dough forms. Grease bottom of a 3 1/2 quart (3.5 L) slow cooker. Turn dough into slow cooker and lay 5 paper towels between top of slow cooker and lid. Put a wooden match or an object 1/8 inch (3 mm) thick between paper towels and edge of slow cooker to allow a bit of steam to escape. Cook on High for about 2 hours. Do not lift lid for the first 1 3/4 hours of cooking time. Loosen sides with a knife. Turn out onto a rack to cool. Cuts into 16 slices.

1 slice: 110 Calories; 2 g Total Fat (1 g Mono, 0.5 g Poly, 0 g Sat); 0 mg Cholesterol; 20 g Carbohydrate (0 g Fibre, 2 g Sugar); 3 g Protein; 150 mg Sodium

Brown Quick bread

This bread is really more like a biscuit. It makes a great mealtime or coffee break treat.

Whole wheat flour	2 cups	500 mL
All-purpose flour	1 cup	250 mL
Baking powder	1 tbsp.	15 mL
Salt	1 tsp.	5 mL
Molasses (not blackstrap)	2 tbsp.	30 mL
Cooking oil	2 tbsp.	30 mL
Water	1 1/3 cups	325 mL

Combine first 4 ingredients in a bowl.

Add molasses, cooking oil and water and mix until moistened. Turn into a greased 5 quart (5 L) slow cooker and place 5 paper towels between top of slow cooker and lid. Put a wooden match or an object 1/8 inch (3 mm) thick between paper towels and edge of slow cooker to allow a bit of steam to escape. Cook on High for about 2 hours. Do not lift lid for the first 1 3/4 hours cooking time. Loosen sides with a knife. Turn out onto a rack to cool. Cuts into 14 wedges.

1 wedge: 120 Calories; 2.5 g Total Fat (1 g Mono, 0.5 g Poly, 0 g Sat); 0 mg Cholesterol; 22 g Carbohydrate (2 g Fibre, 2 g Sugar); 3 g Protein; 230 mg Sodium

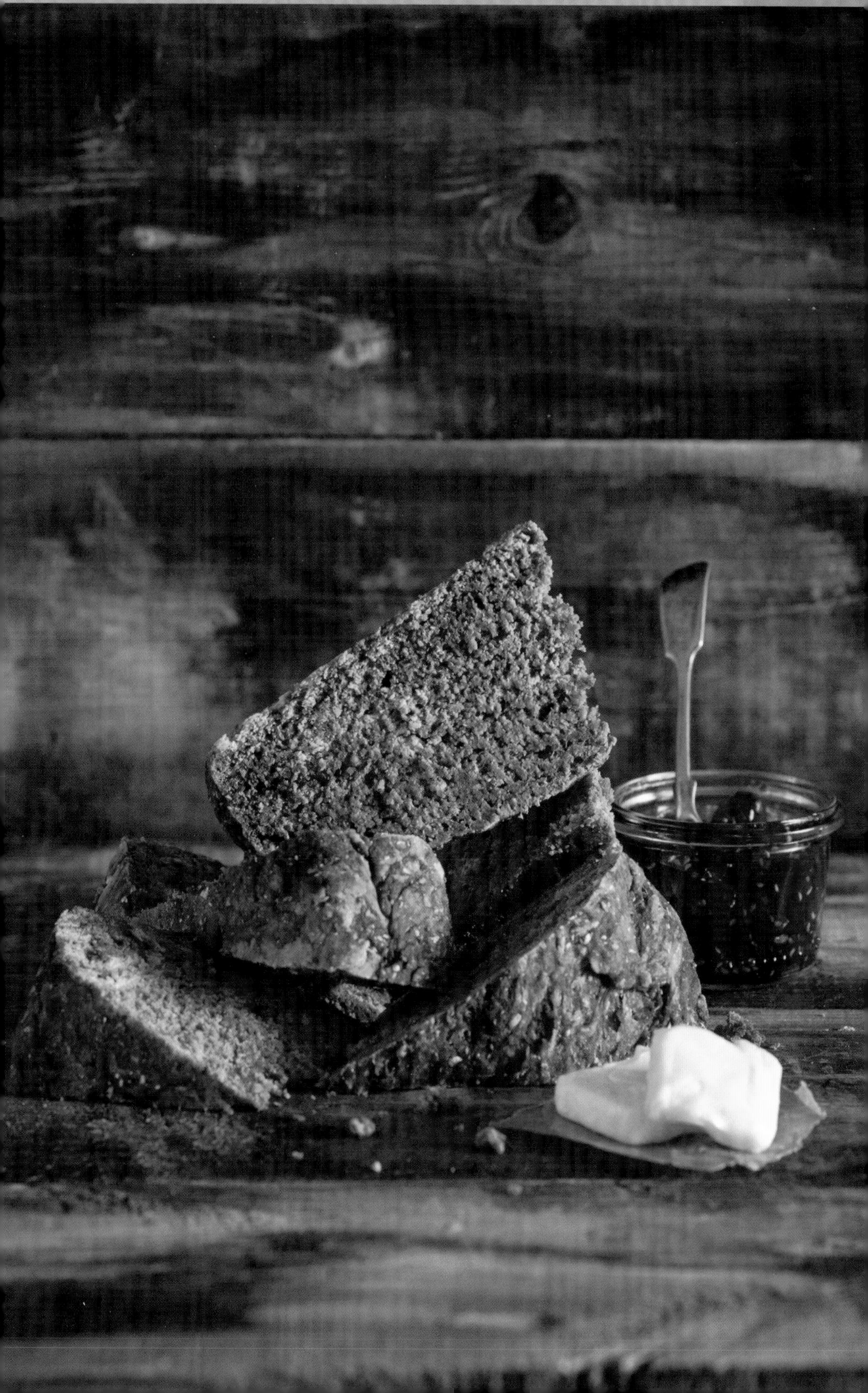

Herb Bread

This bread is a perfect accompaniment to a bowl of chili or stew.

Granulated sugar	1 tsp.	5 mL
Warm water	1 1/3 cups	325 mL
Envelope active dry yeast (1/4 oz., 8 g)	1	1
(1 scant tbsp., 15 mL)		
All-purpose flour	2 cups	500 mL
Granulated sugar	1 tbsp.	15 mL
Cooking oil	2 tbsp.	30 mL
Dried whole oregano	1 tsp.	5 mL
Ground sage	1 tsp.	5 mL
Garlic powder	1/4 tsp.	1 mL
Onion powder	1/4 tsp.	1 mL
Salt	1 tsp.	5 mL
All-purpose flour	1 cup	250 mL

Stir first amount of sugar in warm water in a large warmed bowl. Sprinkle with yeast and let stand for 10 minutes. Stir to dissolve yeast.

Add next 8 ingredients and beat on low to moisten. Beat on medium for 2 minutes.

Work in second amount of flour. Turn into a greased 3 1/2 quart (3.5 L) slow cooker and smooth top with a wet spoon or hand. Place 5 paper towels between top of slow cooker and lid. Put wooden match or an object 1/8 inch (3 mm) thick between paper towels and edge of slow cooker to allow a bit of steam to escape. Do not lift lid for the first 2 hours cooking time. Cook on High for about 2 1/2 hours. Loosen sides with a knife. Turn out onto a rack to cool. Cuts into 14 slices.

1 slice: 120 Calories; 2.5 g Total Fat (1 g Mono, 0.5 g Poly, 0 g Sat); 0 mg Cholesterol; 22 g Carbohydrate (2 g Fibre, 2 g Sugar); 3 g Protein; 230 mg Sodium

Zucchini Cheddar Bacon Bread

A dense, moist bread with delicious bacon bites—another way to use up garden zucchini! Serve with soup for lunch or a light dinner.

All-purpose flour	1 cup	250 mL
Whole wheat flour	1 cup	250 mL
Grated sharp Cheddar cheese	1/4 cup	60 mL
Baking powder	2 tsp.	10 mL
Baking soda	1/2 tsp.	2 mL
Salt	1/4 tsp.	1 mL
Pepper	1/4 tsp.	1 mL
Large eggs, fork-beaten	2	2
Grated zucchini (with peel)	1 1/2 cups	375 mL
Buttermilk (or soured milk, see Tip 1, below)	3/4 cup	175 mL
Bacon slices, cooked crisp and crumbled	2	2
Canola oil	2 tbsp.	30 mL
Thinly sliced green onion	2 tbsp.	30 mL
Boiling water	2 cups	500 mL

Combine first 7 ingredients in a large bowl. Make a well in centre.

Combine next 6 ingredients in a medium bowl. Add to well and stir until just moistened. Spread evenly in a greased 8 inch (20 cm) springform pan. Put an even layer (2 to 3 inches, 5 to 7.5 cm, thick) of crumpled foil into bottom of a 5 to 7 quart (5 to 7 L) slow cooker (see Tip 2, below). Pour boiling water into slow cooker. Place pan on foil, pushing down gently to settle evenly. Place double layer of tea towels over slow cooker liner. Cover with lid and cook on High for about 2 1/2 hours until wooden pick inserted in centre comes out clean. Transfer pan to a wire rack. Cool. Cuts into 12 wedges.

1 wedge: 130 Calories; 4.5 g Total Fat (2 g Mono, 1 g Poly, 1.5 g Sat); 40 mg Cholesterol; 17 g Carbohydrate (2 g Fibre, 1 g Sugar); 5 g Protein; 150 mg Sodium

Tip 1: To make soured milk, pour 1 tbsp. (15 mL) white vinegar or lemon juice into a 1 cup (250 mL) liquid measure. Add enough milk to make 1 cup (250 mL). Stir. Let stand for 1 minute.

Tip 2: Instead of using crumpled foil to elevate pans and other items, you cn use canning jar lids or a roasting rack that fits in your slow cooker.

Lemon Loaf

Light and buttery with a delicate lemon flavour. A perfect match for vanilla ice cream, or sprinkle icing sugar over top of the cooked cake for an attractive presentation.

Ingredient	Imperial	Metric
All-purpose flour	2 cups	500 mL
Baking powder	1 1/4 tsp.	6 mL
Salt	1/2 tsp.	2 mL
Butter (or hard margarine), softened	1/2 cup	125 mL
Granulated sugar	1 cup	250 mL
Large eggs	3	3
Milk	1/2 cup	125 mL
Grated lemon zest	1 1/2 tbsp.	25 mL
Lemon juice	1/4 cup	60 mL
Icing (confectioner's) sugar	1/2 cup	60 mL

Combine first 3 ingredients in a medium bowl. Set aside.

Cream butter and sugar in a large bowl. Add eggs 1 at a time, beating well after each addition.

Add flour mixture in 3 parts, alternating with milk in 2 parts, stirring after each addition until just combined. Add lemon zest. Stir until just combined.

Line bottom of 4 quart (4 L) round slow cooker with foil. Pour batter over foil. Place 5 paper towels between top of slow cooker and lid. Put wooden match or an object 1/8 inch (3 mm) thick between paper towels and edge of slow cooker to allow a bit of steam to escape. Do not lift lid for at least 2 hours. Cook on High for about 2 1/2 hours until wooden pick inserted in center comes out clean. Remove slow cooker liner to rack or turn slow cooker off. Let stand, uncovered, for 20 minutes. Loosen sides of cake with knife. Invert cake onto plate, foil side up, then onto rack, foil side down, to cool. Remove foil before serving.

For the glaze, stir lemon juice into icing sugar in a small bowl until smooth. Randomly poke several holes in loaf with a wooden pick. Spoon lemon juice mixture over hot loaf. Let stand in pan until cooled completely. Cuts into 16 slices.

1 slice: 130 Calories; 1 g Total Fat (0 g Mono, 0 g Poly, 0 g Sat); 40 mg Cholesterol; 26 g Carbohydrate (0 g Fibre, 14 g Sugar); 3 g Protein; 115 mg Sodium

LEMON BLUEBERRY LOAF: Fold in 1 cup (250 mL) fresh (or frozen) blueberries when adding zest until just combined. Bake as directed for 60 to 65 minutes.

LEMON POPPY SEED LOAF: Add 2 tbsp. (30 mL) poppy seeds to flour mixture. Bake as directed.

Graham Crumb Cake

In this unique cake the graham crumbs take the place of flour, giving it a chewy texture. The icing has a nice butterscotch flavour. Garnish with fresh berries for an attractive presentation.

Butter (or hard margarine), softened	1/2 cup	125 mL
Granulated sugar	3/4 cup	175 mL
Large eggs	2	2
Graham cracker crumbs	2 1/4 cups	560 mL
Medium coconut	1/2 cup	125 mL
Baking powder	1 1/2 tsp.	7 mL
Salt	1/8 tsp.	0.5 mL
Milk	1/2 cup	125 mL
Vanilla	1 tsp.	5 mL
Brown sugar, packed	6 tbsp.	90 mL
Milk (or cream)	2 1/2 tbsp.	37 mL
Butter (or hard margarine)	3 tbsp.	45 mL
Icing (confectioner's) sugar	1 1/4 cups	300 mL

Cream butter and sugar together in a bowl. Beat in eggs, 1 at a time. Add graham crumbs, coconut, baking powder and salt. Stir well.

Stir in milk and vanilla. Line bottom of greased 5 quart (5 L) round slow cooker with foil. Pour batter over foil. Place 5 paper towels between top of slow cooker and lid. Put wooden match or an object 1/8 inch (3 mm) thick between paper towels and edge of slow cooker to allow a bit of steam to escape. Do not lift lid. Cook on High for 2 hours until wooden pick inserted in center comes out clean. Remove slow cooker liner to rack or turn slow cooker off. Let stand for 20 minutes. Loosen sides of cake with knife. Invert cake onto plate, foil side up, then onto rack, foil side down, to cool. Remove foil before serving.

For the icing, combine brown sugar, milk and butter in a saucepan. Heat, stirring, until boiling. Boil for 2 minutes. Remove from heat, and set aside to cool.

Add icing sugar. Beat until smooth, adding more milk or icing sugar, if needed, to make proper spreading consistency. Ice top and sides of cake. Cuts into 12 wedges.

1 wedge: 310 Calories; 14 g Total Fat (3 g Mono, 0.5 g Poly, 8 g Sat); 65 mg Cholesterol; 44 g Carbohydrate (1 g Fibre, 33 g Sugar); 3 g Protein; 300 mg Sodium

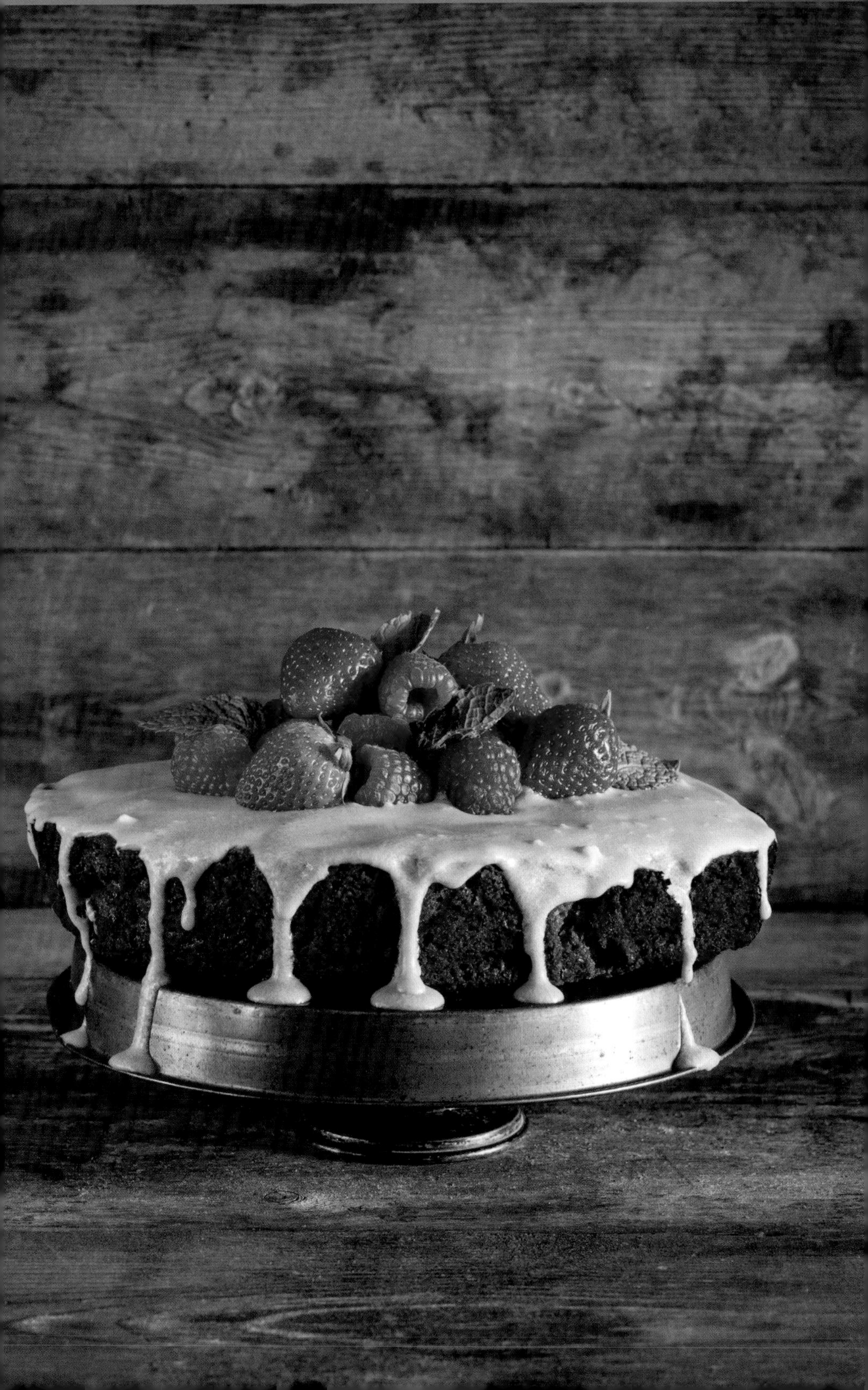

Chocolate Fudge Pudding Cake

No need to heat up the kitchen to enjoy this yummy dessert. Top with whipped cream for an extra decadent dessert.

All-purpose flour	1 cup	250 mL
Brown sugar, packed	3/4 cup	175 mL
Cocoa, sifted if lumpy	2 tbsp.	30 mL
Baking powder	2 tsp.	10 mL
Salt	1/4 tsp.	1 mL
Milk	1/2 cup	125 mL
Cooking oil	2 tbsp.	30 mL
Vanilla extract	1/2 tsp.	2 mL
Brown sugar, packed	3/4 cup	175 mL
Cocoa, sifted if lumpy	2 tbsp.	30 mL
Hot water	1 3/4 cups	425 mL

Combine first 5 ingredients in a medium bowl. Make a well in centre.

Stir next 3 ingredients in a small bowl. Add to well and stir gently until combined. Turn into your slow cooker.

Combine second amounts of brown sugar and cocoa in a separate small bowl. Stir in hot water and pour carefully over batter in slow cooker. Do not stir. Cook on High for about 2 hours until wooden pick inserted in centre comes out clean. Makes 6 servings.

1 serving: 340 Calories; 5 g Total Fat (3 g Mono, 1.5 g Poly, 1 g Sat); 0 mg Cholesterol; 73 g Carbohydrate (2 g Fibre, 54 g Sugar); 4 g Protein; 230 mg Sodium

Brown Betty

Though this dish is typically cooked in the oven, it also works well in the slow cooker.

Medium cooking apples, peeled, cored and sliced (such as McIntosh)	4	4
Brown sugar, packed	3/4 cup	175 mL
Quick-cooking rolled oats (not instant)	1/3 cup	75 mL
All-purpose flour	1/2 cup	125 mL
Salt	1/4 tsp.	1 mL
Butter (or hard margarine), softened	1/3 cup	75 mL

Place apple slices in 3 1/2 quart (3.5 L) slow cooker.

Mix remaining 5 ingredients in a bowl until crumbly. Sprinkle over apple. Place 5 paper towels between top of slow cooker and lid. Put a wooden match between paper towels and edge of slow cooker to allow a bit of steam to escape. Cook on High for 1 1/2 to 2 hours. Makes 4 servings.

1 serving: 430 Calories; 16 g Total Fat (4 g Mono, 1 g Poly, 10 g Sat); 40 mg Cholesterol; 73 g Carbohydrate (3 g Fibre, 53 g Sugar); 3 g Protein; 270 mg Sodium

Mulled Wine

As it cooks, this wine will fill your home with the scent of Christmas. The perfect warming drink for a cold winters day.

Dry red (or alcohol-free) wine	8 cups	2 L
Liquid honey	2/3 cup	150 mL
Cinnamon sticks (4 inches, 10 cm, each in length), broken up and crushed in a plastic bag	3	3
Whole allspice	1 tsp.	5 mL
Whole cloves	1 tsp.	5 mL
Medium orange, sliced	1	1
Lemon juice	1 tsp.	5 mL
Prepared orange juice (or cranberry cocktail)	2 cups	500 mL

Combine wine and honey in a 3 1/2 quart (3.5 L) slow cooker.

Tie cinnamon, allspice and cloves in a double layer of cheesecloth. Add to slow cooker.

Add remaining 3 ingredients. Cook, covered, on Low for at least 3 hours. Discard spice bag. Discard orange slices if desired. Makes 9 cups (2.25 L).

1 cup (250 mL): 270 Calories; 0 g Total Fat (0 g Mono, 0 g Poly, 0 g Sat); 0 mg Cholesterol; 32 g Carbohydrate (0 g Fibre, 26 g Sugar); 3 g Protein; 270 mg Sodium

Hot Buttered Rum

Winter's bone-chilling cold and blustery winds don't seem so terrible when you have this delicious hot toddy to look forward to.

Water	12 cups	3 L
Rum	2 cups	500 mL
Brown sugar, packed	1/2 cup	125 mL
Butter, (or hard margarine)	1/4 cup	60 mL
Ground cinnamon	1/4 tsp.	1 mL
Ground nutmeg	1/4 tsp.	1 mL
Ground cloves	1/8 tsp.	0.5 mL
Salt	1/16 tsp.	0.5 mL

Combine all 8 ingredients in 5 quart (5 L) slow cooker and stir well. Cook, covered, on Low for at least 3 hours until quite warm. Makes 13 cups (3.25 L).

1 cup (250 mL): 140 Calories; 3.5 g Total Fat (1 g Mono, 0 g Poly, 2.5 g Sat); 10 mg Cholesterol; 8 g Carbohydrate (0 g Fibre, 8 g Sugar); 0 g Protein; 40 mg Sodium

Index

Slow Cooker
Favourites

Paré • Darcy

Distributed by
Canada Book Distributors
11414-119 Street
Edmonton. Alberta, Canada T5G 2X6
Tel: 1-800-661-9017

Library and Archives Canada Cataloguing in Publication

Paré, Jean, author
  Slow cooker favourites / Paré, Darcy.

Includes index.
ISBN 978-1-77207-051-4 (softcover)

  1. Electric cooking, Slow. 2. Cookbooks. I. Darcy, James, 1956–, author II. Title. III. Title: At head of title: Company's Coming.

TX827.P3695 2019   641.5'884   C2018-905688-6

All inside photos by Company's coming except: from Sandy Weatherall, 5, 9, 11, 31, 33, 35, 21, 51, 57, 65, 71, 117, 139, 141, 143, 149. From gettyimages: ALLEKO, front cover, 53, 87; Ann_Zhuravleva, background, 123; Bartosz Luczak, 1, 131; bhofack2, 15, 111, 157; bonchan, 45; chas53, 75; cobraphoto, 63; Devrim_PINAR, 7; Diana Taliun, 129; edoneil, 153; EzumeImages, 47; istetiana, 39; ivanmateev, 97; juliedeshaies, 137; Jupiterimages, 113; margouillatphotos, 101; Maria_Lapina, 41; MarianVejcik, 59; Mariha-kitchen, 43; Matt-Brennan, 151; matt6t6, 160; megatronservizi, 147; mg7, 29; Mizina, 17; NatashaBreen, 55; nata_vkusidey, 91; ricardobeenen, 115; robynmac, 6; Saddako, 19; Tanya_F, 127; vanillla, 89; violleta, 105; voltan1, 69; YelenaYemchuk, 79, 81.

We acknowledge the financial support of the Government of Canada.
Nous reconnaissons l'appui financier du gouvernement du Canada.

Funded by the Government of Canada
Financé par le gouvernement du Canada | Canadä

PC: 38